Crisis and Emergency Management and Preparedness for the African-American Church Community

Crisis and Emergency Management and Preparedness for the African-American Church Community

Biblical Application from a Theological Perspective

GEORGE O'NEIL URQUHART

WIPF & STOCK · Eugene, Oregon

CRISIS AND EMERGENCY MANAGEMENT AND PREPAREDNESS
FOR THE AFRICAN-AMERICAN CHURCH COMMUNITY
Biblical Application from a Theological Perspective

Copyright © 2014 George O'Neil Urquhart. All rights reserved. Except for brief quotations in critical publications or reviews, no part of this book may be reproduced in any manner without prior written permission from the publisher. Write: Permissions. Wipf and Stock Publishers, 199 W. 8th Ave., Suite 3, Eugene, OR 97401.

Wipf and Stock
An Imprint of Wipf and Stock Publishers
199 W. 8th Ave., Suite 3
Eugene, OR 97401

www.wipfandstock.com

ISBN 13: 978-1-62564-240-0

Manufactured in the U.S.A.   07/23/2014

To my wife, Jeanetter Maxcean Luster

Contents

Acknowledgments | ix
Preface | xiii
Glossary | xvi

Introduction: "The Word Is Out: It Is No Secret" | 1

1 **Ministry Focus:** Consider the Warning | 10

2 **The State of the Art of This Model for Ministry:**
A Preparedness Posture | 26

3 **Theoretical Foundations for the Model:**
Methodology for Finding Safety in the Sanctuary | 44

4 **Engaging the Task and Assigning Responsibilities:**
Field Experience | 72

5 **Summary, Reflections, and Conclusions** | 93

Appendix: Model Emergency Management and Preparedness Planning | 101

Bibliography | 115

Acknowledgments

FIRST, I THANK ALMIGHTY God for the graciousness of life and for divine guidance and preparation for this project. This endeavor is a product of myriad experiences, including years of training and wisdom shared by my elders and a host of contemporaries. Several persons in the vocation of emergency management and preparedness and members of the clergy profession were introduced to this initiative and have since become consultative or signatory partners to the project. Without exception each person has offered individual resources and collectively demonstrated a keen sense of the context of the work. I want to thank particularly the team of Contextual Associates, which, without hesitation, volunteered to provide helpful insights and resources to this project.

The project could not have proceeded as designed were it not for the inspired guidance of my academic advisor, Dr. Mary H. Young, EdD, associate dean at Samuel DeWitt Proctor School of Theology, Virginia Union University, who encouraged me to limit the scope of this particular endeavor and focus primarily on the development of an emergency management and preparedness plan for a typical African American church. In this regard I thank the congregation of the Providence Park Baptist Church, Richmond, Virginia, the target audience, which, with the leadership and support of its pastor Dr. Jerome Clayton Ross, PhD, offered to help explore and validate the project as a practical model for any African American church or similar organization. Also, I thank Providence Park Baptist Church for use of its facilities and resources that have contributed to this project. Again, thanks

Acknowledgments

to Pastor Ross, other members of the church leadership, and the congregation at large for welcoming my wife and me to this fellowship and for granting me the privilege of serving on the Board of Christian Education (BCE) as one of its co-chairs.

I want to thank the Baptist General Convention of Virginia (BGCVA) for being sensitive to the need for emergency preparedness for its affiliated associations and church bodies. Working through and with the assistance of Dr. J. Elisha Burke, the BGCVA invited and afforded me the opportunity to introduce this project during its early stage to the BGCVA leadership and to subsequently offer guidance and share emergency planning concepts in several of its regional sessions with church leaders and representatives from all across the Commonwealth of Virginia. And special thanks are extended to Rev. Benjamin Campbell, pastoral director at Richmond Hill (VA) Ecumenical Christian Retreat Center, and Reverend Jonathan Barton, general minister of the Virginia Council of Churches, for granting me the privilege of listening to their stories regarding church cooperation and for sharing their emergency preparedness experiences.

I offer my grateful acknowledgment and eternal indebtedness to many federal, state, and local government emergency management professionals with whom I've had the distinct privilege to grow, learn, and share knowledge and skills during thirty-plus years of state service in the profession. The Virginia Department of Emergency Management (VDEM) has been my home office for these many years; and having served in various managerial and leadership capacities, it would be unpardonable to not expose some of the valuable historical and performance-based insights and lessons encountered during that time with the ecclesial community where I am privileged to serve. Visit the VDEM website (www.vaemergency.com) for related information and many helpful resources.

Acknowledgments

    Finally, but certainly not the least, my thanks belong to my wife, Jeanetter Maxcean, who for forty-seven years has tirelessly supported me and given of herself and her voice to the broader endeavor of our joint ministry.

George O'Neil Urquhart
April 2011

Preface

THIS DOCUMENT IS DESIGNED to highlight a perceived need and responsibility by the African American church to address the unique exposure or vulnerability of the African American community in times of a crisis or devastating major emergency. Three areas or focal points are made prominent in this work to help guide the planning process with the intent being preservation of the historically cohesive nature of certain communities at risk. They are (1) to awaken the community to the types of emergencies that are most likely to affect the church or environment, (2) to encourage the church by assisting the respective leadership and members of the congregation to identify and use their gifts and skills in such a manner in which they will have something to contribute to the overall cause in the event of an emergency, and (3) to equip the corporate entity by development and use of an emergency plan, appropriate identification and employment of persons who have the requisite professional background and talents who may be called upon and tasked to offer consultation, and making available training to prepare individuals in the proper response to an emergency should one occur.

Preservation of the historically cohesive nature of the predominantly African American community as used in this document refers to my experience living in the southeast Virginia villages of Newville and Homeville, both locally addressed as Waverly, Virginia. Three predominantly African American Baptist churches serve these two sparsely populated rural neighborhoods that consist of fewer than thirty households spread out over a

Preface

six-mile radius. Not one of these churches could exist alone were it not for members or visitors from outside the local area. Of course each of these churches has its familial and unique constituents; yet the overall community is severely challenged to maintain or support broad-scale ministries for the overall health of the church population without the cooperation of the other. At one time all three churches were constituted as a single body; however, over time the original and historic church grew apart for various reasons. I believe similar circumstances exist in other African American communities, and this local example is given primarily as an indicator of the strained historic and cohesive nature of community and what is assumed to exist in other rural as well as some urban congregations.

Emergencies and disasters come in all types and these risks—be they actual or viewed as threats—have demonstrated that they have no respect for boundaries and neither do they have regard for the sacred or secular. The church universal and church local cannot wait or depend on government to be there for them in times of critical need; rather, the church, as surveyed in this context, must identify and make better use of its unique in-house resources and talents. History has shown that the entire region may be severely affected by the catastrophe or a major disaster and the local church and resident community may have to operate and survive on its own for an indefinite period of time until power is restored and the community returns to normalcy. Why wait for a disaster to strike before churches put aside differences and work for a unified purpose? The case is patently clear that Christians, indeed the church, must collaboratively mobilize to meet the challenge of both natural and human-caused disasters.

This document has been prepared for direct and immediate dissemination and use by the African American church community, and any church or community organization, for that matter, in preparing for a crisis or emergency involving the church and the extended resident community. It consists of a model or template of a church emergency preparedness plan patterned after work coordinated, conducted, and completed in conjunction with

Preface

Providence Park Baptist Church, Richmond, Virginia, the target community. The plan is designed to be used to help the church leadership and primary auxiliaries and ministries as well as the congregants to help better prepare for and respond to emergencies that have a high probability of disrupting normal activities and church operations in times of an emergency or crisis event.

Glossary

BGCVA – Baptist General Convention of Virginia. Founded in 1899 to unite and equip churches, ministries, associations, and constituents to do holistic ministry that propagates the gospel, advances the kingdom of God, and supports education and missions in Virginia and beyond.

Catastrophe – Any natural or human-made incident, including acts of terrorism, that results in extraordinary levels of mass casualties, damage, or disruption severely affecting the population, infrastructure, environment, economy, and/or government functions.

CEMP – Crisis and Emergency Management Preparedness. Emergency planning, exercises, training, and resource development are elements of CEMP.

Continuity of Operations – A process of identifying the essential functions—including staff, systems, and procedures—that ensure the continuation of a church's ability to function or operate.

Glossary

Coordination – The process of systemically analyzing a situation, developing relevant information, and informing appropriate personnel of viable alternatives for selection of the most effective combination of available resources to meet specific objectives.

CPR/AED – Cardio Pulmonary Resuscitation and Automatic External Defibrillator.

Crisis – A situation that somehow challenges the public's sense of appropriateness, tradition, values, safety, security, or the integrity of the entity or organization, whether by fear of unknown consequences, terror, etc.

Declaration of Emergency – Whenever the church leadership (pastor or other chief official) determines that the safety and welfare of the congregation or user groups of the church require the exercise of extreme emergency measures.

Disaster – 1. Any human-caused situation, including any condition following an attack by any enemy or foreign nation upon the United States, resulting in substantial damage of property or injury to persons in the United States. Such a disaster may result from use of bombs, missiles, or shell fire; nuclear, radiological, chemical, or biological means; other weapons; overt paramilitary actions; terrorism, both foreign and domestic; and also any industrial, nuclear, or transportation accident, such as explosion, conflagration, power failure, resource shortage; or other conditions such as sabotage, oil spills, and other injurious environmental contaminations that threaten or cause damage to property, human suffering, hardship, or loss of life.

Glossary

2. Any natural disaster, including any hurricane, tornado, storm, flood, high water, wind-driven water, tidal wave, earthquake, drought, fire, communicable disease or public health threat, or other natural catastrophe resulting in damage, hardship, suffering, or possible loss of life.

Emergency – Any occurrence, or threat thereof, whether natural or human-made, that results or may result in substantial injury or harm to the population or substantial damage to or loss of property or natural resources, and may involve governmental action beyond that authorized or contemplated by existing law or because governmental inaction for the period required to amend the law to meet the exigency would work immediate and irrevocable harm upon the citizens or the environment or some clearly defined portion or portions thereof.

Emergency Management – An entity or organization with a primary mission of dealing with preparation for and the carrying out of functions to prevent, minimize, and repair injury and damage resulting from natural or human-made disasters. These functions include communications, such as alerting, notification, and warning; evacuation; facility protection; fire detection and prevention; medical and health; restoration of services; safety and security; and other functions related to preserving health, safety, and welfare.

Emergency Plan – A document that provides for a preplanned and coordinated response in the event of an emergency or disaster situation.

Emergency Support Function – A function that requires or involves a key individual or select ministry to provide or to coordinate certain resources in response to emergencies or disasters.

Glossary

Evacuation – Assisting people to move from the path or threat of a disaster to an area of relative safety.

Exercise – An activity designed to promote emergency preparedness; test or evaluate emergency operations plans, procedures, or facilities; train personnel in emergency response duties; and demonstrate operational capability.

FEMA – Federal Emergency Management Agency, the federal agency that offers aid to disaster victims, including individuals, state and local governments, tribes, and other not-for-profit organizations. FEMA is a key agency under the umbrella of the U.S. Department of Homeland Security.

Incident – An occurrence or event, natural or human-caused, that requires an emergency response to protect life or property.

Incident Coordinator – The individual responsible for the management of all incident operations.

Mitigation – Activities that actually eliminate or reduce the chance occurrence, reoccurrence, or the effects of a disaster.

Mutual Aid Agreement – A written agreement between agencies and/or churches in which they agree to assist one another, upon request, by furnishing facilities, personnel, and equipment in an emergency situation. The term Memorandum of Understanding (MOU) is sometimes used interchangeably.

PPBC – Providence Park Baptist Church, the constituent target community incorporated in this project. Established in 1876, it is located at 468 East Ladies Mile Road, Richmond, Virginia.

Glossary

Preparedness – A system of functions that includes the development of plans and related components to ensure the most effective, efficient response to a disaster or emergency. Preparedness activities are designed to help save lives and minimize damage by preparing organizations and people to respond appropriately when an emergency is imminent. Preparedness also includes conducting training and exercises and establishing resources necessary to achieve readiness for all hazards. It is a function that embraces and requires leadership, training, readiness, and support to recognize, prevent, and react to an emergency.

Recovery – Activities that address the short-term and long-term needs and the resources to assist, restore, strengthen, and rebuild affected properties, etc.

Response – Activities that address the short-term, direct effects of an incident. Response includes immediate actions to save lives, protect property, and meet basic human needs.

Threat – Any indication of possible violence, harm, or danger.

VDEM – Virginia Department of Emergency Management, the agency of the Commonwealth of Virginia with the mission to protect the lives and property of Virginia's citizens from emergencies and disasters by coordinating the state's emergency preparedness, mitigation, response, and recovery efforts.

Volunteer – An individual accepted to perform services by the church without promise, expectation, or receipt of compensation for services performed.

Introduction

"The Word Is Out: It Is No Secret"

DURING MY CAREER AND while surveying the community and environment from a disaster preparedness perspective, I sense an urgent need and detect a tremendous gap in the area of resources and skills among and within certain enterprises and institutions, and especially among and within most churches, where seemingly they are grossly unprepared to deal with a major emergency or disaster. We must heed the call to action and respond with appropriate action and wisdom of the heart. This is part of our being human. A psychiatrist once noted that "being human means being confronted continually with situations, each of which is at once a chance and a challenge, giving us a 'chance' to fulfill ourselves by meeting the 'challenge' to fulfill its meaning. Each situation is a call, first to listen, and then to respond."[1] Thus, one must always listen attentively and patiently to the voice within and respond accordingly.

Statement of the Problem

The project primarily deals with the subject of *Crisis and Emergency Management and Preparedness for the African American Church Community*. It is without question that all communities, including our churches, are vulnerable to any number of risks

1. Frankl, *Man's Search for Ultimate Meaning*, 126.

and threats—from natural disasters, human-made incidents, pandemic disease outbreaks, violence resulting from terrorism from abroad as well as homegrown within our neighborhoods, and the growing menace of localized cultural and social disorders. We need to be prepared, and the time is now! In this document, I will address emergency preparedness for all hazards (see the Glossary definition for *disaster*).

Problem Resolution

The specific focus and outcomes of this project will be to (1) highlight the risks that may affect Providence Park Baptist Church, the target community; (2) engage a planning model that focuses on awakening or awareness, encouragement, and equipping as a means of preparing the community for disasters and emergencies; and (3) develop an emergency plan for the target church.

The resident population served by the predominantly African American church demands and deserves specific attention to preserve the uniquely cohesive nature of the African American community, especially in these times of great challenge, stress, and vulnerability. While the project may ultimately have some validity beyond the specific confines of the target community, there is a shared hope among the immediate audience that the success of the endeavor may help mitigate growing environmental and social concerns beyond traditional emergencies—floods, hurricanes, tornadoes, severe weather, power outages—imposed on communities already strained by economic and social inequities.

Passion for Emergency Preparedness Ministry

My passion for this project was born out of a conversation I had with an emergency management colleague in 1984. The focus of the dialogue centered on the question: to what extent does human behavior contribute to natural disasters? We sought to make sense out of the question by looking at the physical makeup of

Introduction

the human anatomy, that is, from our understanding that persons give off positive energy and negative energy depending on one's mood or the condition of the heart, the center of emotion. Human emotions and intentions, we concluded, combine to produce the motivating force that drives or manifests outward action, and by so doing creates energy and tension. That energy gives off heat and, thus influences one's space and his or her surroundings. The environment created becomes positively or negatively charged depending on the motivating force. When energies collide—positive or negative—they create a stable or unstable environment. Stated in another way, the energy field of one person will be one such that another person either will be attracted to or will resist with an equal amount of energy—similar to the effect produced by a zone of good karma or bad karma. Tensions are created when individuals are at odds. Taken to another level or viewed from another perspective, positive and negative energies, when released in the environment, create static and form a mass that, when joined with the natural elements or forces of nature, create clouds. From our physics classes we knew that clouds have the potential to produce thunder, lightning, rain, or other forms of precipitation. Depending on the energy field or source, the atmospheric mass produced could be relatively small compared with normal cloud formations. What happens after that is anyone's opinion. We knew that we were in unchartered waters by having such a conversation, however plausible the argument appeared to be. That line of reasoning was about the extent of a range of related questions that would pique our interest more than once. The notion that human behavior has the ability to affect the course of nature continues to engage my senses with uncanny inquisitiveness.

Being a person of faith then as now, and as to be expected during the course of my sojourn in the field of theology at the Samuel DeWitt Proctor School of Theology at Virginia Union University, I became very interested in the study of theodicy, that is, a search to answer the foregoing question or determine to what extent God deals with the presence of evil and ungodly acts in the universe. Often during my career in public safety and emergency management, and being confronted with the human dimensions of tragedy caused by hurricanes, floods, tornadoes, and so forth, I was often asked and wanted to supply a reasoned answer to the question of why a given devastation occurred. As will be discussed later in chapter 3, it has been discovered that human behavior—though not without some suspicion—is a major contributor to the condition of the earth's natural order of being by virtue of human enterprise in a business and industrial global world climate. While that finding may have some validity and may shed light on a subject that may elude the most ardent researcher, I knew it was an idea that would take me on a tangent far away from a pragmatic approach to emergency management and preparedness. Whatever the reasoning or source of disasters and emergencies, I knew that the appropriate and expedient thing to do was to embrace a practice as consistent as possible with the purpose of God working in and through the various ambiguities of human activity.

There are no fail-safe or objective answers to the cause of disasters, be they human caused or natural. Nevertheless, what church leaders and churches as a whole can do is hope. Hope does not disappoint. A sage of old exhorted listeners to "hope in God" (Ps 42:5, 11). The writer of the scriptural letters to the Romans (8:24–25), Corinthians (1 Cor. 13:7), Ephesians (2:8), and Hebrews (11:1) urged those respective audiences to take courage in the knowledge that there is salvation in hope and to be faithful in their calling, knowing that hope accompanies salvation and hope never fails. Moreover, because hope is not passive but rather active, hope engenders rightful action based on the urging of the heart, as I discuss at some length in chapters 1 and 2.

To further introduce the audience and reader to the project at hand and to clarify my primary intent, I leave the subject of theodicy and the matter of causality of disasters and turn to the question of what should our response to the reality of disasters be. What this means is that we—in this case, the church, and more specifically to this project, the African American church—must develop a practical, all-hazards emergency preparedness plan, allocate appropriate resources for its success, and follow the plan as

Introduction

an unmistakable blueprint to help secure our future. The title of this project is "Crisis and Emergency Management and Preparedness for the African American Church Community," where the target church will serve as the primary focus for development and implementation of the subject plan in time of need.

The assets I bring and offer to the Doctor of Ministry Program at Samuel DeWitt Proctor School of Theology of Virginia Union University (STVU) will hopefully occasion and present new avenues of outreach for the School of Theology at Virginia Union and position STVU as an innovator and major contributor to the area of emergency preparedness and life safety for the local church. In addition to the primary project, the prospect for a future STVU-approved and customized curriculum on emergency management and preparedness for the African American church community should prove timely and extremely useful in advance of ever-increasing emergencies and disasters with potentially catastrophic and devastating results. The work will be a shared project where all parties will be given the opportunity to establish ownership as stakeholders in the end results.

There is an overwhelming need for the development of the CEMP project for churches. Standing in the face of economic and social threats and situated on the banks of potential disasters of one type or the other, we must move beyond apathy, defeatism, and pessimism to a new level of awareness, intelligence, preparedness, and resourcefulness. Should we fail to plan, we will surely plan to fail. Churches in African American neighborhoods are considerably more vulnerable to the dreadful consequences of disasters and emergencies, in large measure because of their unique congregational requirements, location, and resource commitments, which perhaps differ from some other communities. This problem or perception of such is exacerbated by and becoming more acute because of the fragmentation of congregations, groundless difference of opinions, and passive reliance on local, state, and/or federal government programs.

Absent collaboration and cooperation among the local churches, the predominantly African American church will be less

Crisis and Emergency Management and Preparedness

effective in helping its membership in the event of an emergency. And should there be a disaster in the area, most churches, almost without exception—if operating or relying solely on its own capabilities and resources—will be found powerless and, worst of all, be discovered among the victims rather than within the cadre of helpers. Yung Suk Kim, author of *Christ's Body in Corinth*, writes that "today, God calls people to work for a livable, peaceful world full of diversity and differences."[2] In defining the conditions and elements in the church community, Professor Kim concludes his investigation by offering a range of considerations aimed at building bridges where relations between churches have become strained. He suggests that people called by God need to create more room for true dialogue between cultures, banish the act and thought of irresponsible individualism, respect differences, engage the other with self-critical awareness, and care for the other in solidarity and for creation and wonder. Looking ahead without access to broad-based collegial and cooperative ventures among and within the African American churches, one by one the traditional African American church will cease to exist as a thriving or vibrant resource for a struggling community.

Emergency management and preparedness requires competent leadership foremost. A leader of any people must be a servant, and thus the care of them will be rendered in a servant-leadership manner consistent with the prevailing culture, passion, or personality. Ultimately, the leader's effectiveness will be a function of his or her ability to navigate challenging or difficult situations in proportion to the demonstrated consent or willingness of those who are persuaded or resigned to follow the servant's lead.

In an effort to further develop, enhance, and equip the churches, I have identified and will continue to work with the Baptist General Convention of Virginia (BGCVA), the Tuckahoe Baptist Association, other associations, and Providence Park Baptist Church to help satisfy ministry obligations to the community in the area of emergency management and preparedness. The goal and success of this project will be the implementation of a viable

---

2. Kim, *Christ's Body In Corinth*, 102.

Introduction

emergency preparedness management orientation program for the BGCVA and a model Crisis And Emergency Management And Preparedness (CEMP) plan using Providence Park Baptist Church, Richmond, as the target community. See chapter 3 for a discussion of the project methodology.

I am proposing a model CEMP plan that may be offered and replicated by African American congregations and other church communities across Virginia and beyond. The Commonwealth of Virginia has made great strides in emergency management and is nationally recognized for its emergency management and preparedness program. There is no reason why the broader community and its churches should be any less prepared to model a supportive partnership among and within its congregations. A noted author advises, "Begin preparing now. Don't wait to see what might happen. If you respond in just a few areas, you will be better prepared than you were yesterday. But if you have the foresight to work toward a more comprehensive plan, you will be well prepared for most storms that are thrown at you."[3]

An emergency is an abnormal situation that requires prompt action, beyond normal procedures, to limit damage to persons, property, or the environment. A crisis, on the other hand, is a situation that somehow challenges the public's sense of appropriateness, tradition, values, safety, security, or the integrity of the entity or organization, whether by fear of unknown consequences, terror, and so forth. In his book titled *Crisis Preaching: Personal and Public*, Joseph Jeter raises the question: "What is a crisis?" In response he notes, "R. L. Pavelesky defines crisis as that loss of balance that W. B. Yeats described more poetically: 'Things fall apart; the centre cannot hold.'"[4] Jeter comments on the question from two other sources and writes, "Charles Gerkin describes a crisis as an extreme or boundary condition in which 'the fundamental contradiction between human aspirations and finite possibilities becomes visible in such a way as to demand attention.' Harry Emerson Fosdick defined it in more passionate language:

3. Hanna, *Safe and Secure*, 103.
4. Jeter, *Crisis Preaching*, 13.

Crisis and Emergency Management and Preparedness

> "Deep trouble," we say, not broad, long, high—those adjectives would not apply—but "deep trouble." When the psalmist says, "Out of the depths have I cried unto thee, O Lord," we know what he means. He is in trouble."[5]

Past experiences have demonstrated that emergencies can quickly turn into crises if it appears that government or the responsible entity is not on top of the situation. Although crises and emergencies require different approaches, both types of situations involve many stakeholders and thus represent a tremendous challenge to coordinate the functional requirements of emergency operations and response. And that's why emergency planning is so very essential to systematic emergency management.

Crises and more often emergencies can occur in any area or sector of human activity or endeavor. Unlike emergencies in many respects, crises require action specifically designed to reestablish public confidence and integrity in organizational life. Emergencies involve action to limit damage to people, property, and the environment. In Virginia, we call these two management and operational concepts *crisis* and *consequence*. Crisis looks into the causality of the incident or threat. Consequence is the response to and recovery from the incident.

Emergency management involves collaboration between federal, state, and local government agencies and various professional volunteer organizations. In such a context, the key to a successful response basically relies on the ability of the several stakeholders to coordinate efforts with respect to operations and communications. The purpose of our engagement with the churches is to be aware of this culture and to build or develop the emergency management and preparedness plan within the context of the larger sphere of operations.

Each chapter of this project document is devoted to an essential element of emergency management and preparedness and the context of the overall effort. Chapter 1 presents an overview of my background and motivation for the project. In chapter 2 I examine the state of the art of this model for ministry, that is, to what extent

5. Ibid.

Introduction

an emergency preparedness posture will foster a more holistic approach for dealing with a myriad array of community needs and problems, which is now suggested by some members of the clergy and laity to be an overwhelming concern for churches and the ecclesial community. Next, I turn in chapter 3 to an analysis of the theoretical context of emergency preparedness in light of various theological and social perspectives that provide a bridge or nexus to the project methodology and planning paradigm. In chapter 4 the reader is invited to observe the implementation side of the model. Chapter 5 includes the summary, reflections, and conclusions.

It is my hope that any omissions and opportunities left untapped in this project will provide the forum or platform for follow-up investigations in emergency management and preparedness and demonstrate how the Crisis and Emergency Management and Preparedness (CEMP) model may serve as a bridge to link or network churches where, if united, they may faithfully extend the collective reaches of collaborative life-safety ministries. The ideal model would be a collective emergency management plan for churches that addresses the overall development and enhancement of capabilities and resources to respond appropriately and timely in the event of an emergency or disaster anywhere within the region.

1

Ministry Focus

Consider the Warning

PLATO OBSERVED THAT IT is the *thymoeidés* (that area of one's being that is related to the soul of man, called the spirited, courageous element, that lies between the intellectual and the sensual element in man, and the area that harbors and contemplates the unreflective striving toward what is noble) of human beings that, as an essential function of one's being, is the ethical value and sociological quality.[1] In this chapter my focus will be to present an overview of my background and motivation for the project.

An individual's life journey is characterized and represented by a series of milestones consisting metaphorically of sprints, bounds and leaps, stops and detours, reversals or turnarounds, stumbles and accidental collisions, disappointments and engagements, falls, bruises and bumps, breakdowns, patches and repairs, and, curiously, intersections with other travelers. To make sense out of this collage of demographic and geological adventures and incidents, these happenings must first be tactfully recorded, then bridged or connected to see the tapestry that is being created or inspired.

---

1. Sinani, "Courage to Be in the Philosophy of Paul Tillich."

Ministry Focus

Autobiographical Statement

Introspection and retrospection inform my story. The influence of God-fearing parents and their love of God taught me by example and instruction within the context of loving discipline to trust in the Lord for all things. Their uncompromising dependence on God and their ultimate regard for community, demonstrated by generosity and a courageously intense love for family and church, provided a diverse environment that continues to illumine, nourish, and reverberate within the pulse of my temporal existence. My mother and father, both of whom are deceased, loved and practiced Christian doctrine.

Being born in Sussex County, Virginia, in the early 1940s, a product of that county's segregated primary and elementary school system, has given me the greatest admiration and respect for the parents, teachers, and pastors who were courageous in their leadership and teachings and who sacrificed talents and time for those under their care and tutelage. I remember and recognize now just how much dedication and unselfish devotion these persons shared in community with others in spite of outright intimidation, opposition, and threats to livelihood. Growing up too in a farming community, some eight miles outside of Waverly, the nearest town, instilled in me both materially and mentally the discipline and rewards of character, conservation, humility, and responsibility.

Christ-centered parental training was reinforced and enhanced through extended Christian education and worship experiences. At an early age I was introduced and came to a personal faith and knowledge of the guidance and providence of God. I now understand that these experiences were the beginning moments of truth and the initial phase in the development of statement of faith formations.I received my elementary and secondary education from Sussex County Public Schools and earned a Bachelor of Science degree from Virginia Commonwealth University in 1975, in urban studies and regional planning. In 1980 I received a Master of Arts degree in public administration from the University of Virginia.

Crisis and Emergency Management and Preparedness

My employment and professional history spans a career that includes a wide variety of engagements and tenures, ranging from the educational arena to corporate and public-sector management. Currently employed with the Commonwealth of Virginia, I have served for almost forty years in executive- and senior-level civil service positions, including both corporate and public service. I have been blessed to receive gubernatorial appointments by Governors Charles Robb (1984), Douglas Wilder (1992), George Allen (1995), and James Gilmore (2000).

Civic duties and involvement in social functions have been tremendously helpful and instrumental in the formation of professional development skills. Such open-door privileges have been two-sided: I have come to observe and appreciate the great strides and triumphs of many who were once denied equal access to excellent opportunities; yet, on the other hand—and this is one of the major issues that contributed to my call to the ministry—I have been exposed to the agonizing cries of God's people as they have struggled with trauma and tragedy as a result of institutional inequities and circumstances not of their own choosing. These are distressing tensions on society at large, and I have on more than one occasion confronted and engaged the political and social system to bring attention to and correct such glaring inequalities and injustices.

How I came to enter ministry and become a gospel preacher, however, is the story of a lifetime. My early and young adult years were strongly influenced by the community. The local church and public elementary and high schools helped reinforce home discipline and enlightenment. That extended community would eventually include institutions of higher learning and a workplace that provided opportunities that ultimately challenged childhood presuppositions.

It was, however, the providence of God that led me to become an ordained deacon in July 1978 at Wilborne Baptist Church, Waverly, Virginia. Before my ordination and since, I have endeavored to serve the faith community in a number of lay capacities, from church Sunday school teacher, to school superintendent, to

Ministry Focus

president of the Sussex County Sunday School Union (1991–92), where I afterward served six years as its director of youth ministry. I am a servant of the church of God and am called by God to proclaim the gospel of Jesus Christ. I used to struggle with the question, "Where shall I proclaim the good news of Jesus Christ?" The Word of God came and told me to preach the gospel in whatsoever capacity or place I may be found. Seldom has a day gone by without the opportunity to minister to someone in need, either through a word of wisdom or a helping hand of support through some difficult circumstance.

As noted previously, my theological pilgrimage has been adventuresome by no less than the majesty and mystery of the divine call. This duty of divine discipleship has been characterized by a series of experiences and perspectives that continues to illumine the essence of this pilgrimage and gives light to the actuality of a destination only revealed "little by little" by God. To better understand my theology and Christian pilgrimage, permit me to share a few specific experiences that will help shed light on my educational development and perhaps make this autobiographical statement somewhat more intuitive in the final analysis.

It was no less than a theophanic appearance in the form of a command to "study to show thyself approved unto God" (2 Tim 2:15) that eventually lead me to the School of Theology at Virginia Union University. That was the first clear voice I heard from the Divine Eternal (through the lips of my wife) upon seeking God's guidance relative to the call to the ministry. However, in retrospect, years before my acceptance and public announcement of the call to the ministry of the gospel, many colleagues occasionally referred to me as minister or pastor. In addition to becoming tired of telling them, "No, not me," I was nevertheless often surprised and taken aback when a complete stranger would comment to me or to someone close or near me, "He's [or 'you are'] a preacher." Even as time went on members of the clergy would comment privately to me or publicly state that the Lord has called me/him to preach.

I came to the call after a period in which I came to recognize the precious gift of ministry, a gift that others recognized, confirmed, and affirmed for me. It was through this chain of events that in the summer of 2002 I came to be enrolled in the Master of Divinity program at the Samuel DeWitt Proctor School of Theology, Virginia Union University, to further my growth in the wisdom of God. As part of the continuing affirmation of the call to the gospel ministry, I graduated in May 2005 with a Master of Divinity degree.

As if on dual tracks propelled by prayerful support of others, studying under the likes of the late Miles Jerome Jones (STVU professor of homiletics), and the teaching and urging of the Spirit, I came to preach my inaugural message on March 2, 2003. Called to my first pastorate in February 2010, I was later publicly set apart and ordained to the work of the gospel ministry on April 18, 2010, at Providence Park Baptist Church, Richmond, under the leadership of its pastor, Reverend Jerome C. Ross, PhD. Through patience and the grace of God, I was installed as pastor of Plank Road Baptist Church, Waverly, on May 2, 2010. Wayne Muller sums up the context and essence of our ministerial call with these words: "The opportune moment for kindness and generosity seems to present itself clearly, if only we are able to hear and are prepared to respond."[2]

I soon learned that we cannot ever get to a point and say learning and studying are complete, whatever the field or profession. As faith and time would have it, I made application to the Samuel DeWitt School of Theology, Virginia Union University, in April 2008 to the Doctor of Ministry program. Later, in May 2008, I received an acceptance letter congratulating me and granting me admission to the program beginning September 2008. This project was part of the culmination of the requirements of the Doctor of Ministry degree program from which I graduated in May 2011.

---

2. Muller, *How Then, Shall We Live?*, 276.

Ministry Focus

Continuing the Call

The work of ministry is a calling and life journey. My aim and hope is that I may practice the gospel that is preached, faithfully serve among and with the people of God in the various occupations where I am privileged to serve, and share the gifts and talents in service of the kingdom of God as a disciple of the Master.

In many respects, life is a work of art expressed through the prism of our lives in which we assess and assign meaning and value to activities and adventures, various objects, people and places, and situations. In essence, one's life consists of an array of choices and decisions, accidental and deliberate exchanges and interactions, health conditions, possessions, and acts of God in life and nature. Through these and other experiences, I have arrived at a new destination driven and founded upon the God presence within. This internal and uniquely human endeavor—credited as a phenomenon of a new reality—initially grew out of what appeared to the human eye and consciousness as a failure of the human enterprise, particularly within the African American community to build on successes of the past and capitalize on the opportunities of the present.

Open-door challenges and opportunities for success sometimes seemingly disappear into a future unknown. In my opinion, what appeared to the naked eye was a kind of aimlessness within the African American psyche, an anxiety, sense of despair, denial, and even transference, that is, the problems within the home and neighborhood and other social disorders were manifestations of disparate and unconscionable operative institutions within the American culture or system. Through inspection and reflection, and perhaps a little introspection, I discovered, however, that all is not lost. Regardless of personal context, cause of conditions, problems or situations, social location, or any other alignment or group factors that might help explain what appeared to me as human and systemic failures, there is still hope—a hope that is alive, a hope that may need to be encouraged, prompted, or stirred within community.

Crisis and Emergency Management and Preparedness

Perhaps a story or testimony offered here might help illumine my passion for ministry, give insight to the foregoing, explain current context of ministry, and focus continued work in this area. My initial call to the ministry grew out of the experiences of living in a community that seemed to have lost its way and in some respects appeared to extract or rob people of what would give hope and promise, that is, to give life its ultimate meaning. This appearance-turned discernment continued to drive me to seek answers, both for myself and for the community. During and between the times this book project was taking shape and my travel to work a funny or strange thing happened. I discovered that the Holy Spirit was in control. It is that driving force that may be explained only by one's relationship with the Creator God. Thus began a personal seeking for guidance and wisdom. In other words, I wanted to be helpful; however, I did not know exactly what to do or where to begin.

It is said that there is a religious sense deeply rooted in each person's unconscious depths—that one is driven by an inner presence. The breath of God is the inner being, and this uniquely created understanding within each individual is what drives one to seek to be the creature God created us to be! Two statements have informed my modus operandi in the context of my ministerial and personal life. I found out, in driving from home to work to seminary during that early three-year experience (2002–2005), that it was God's presence that "Carried (Me) by Grace on Wings of Faith."[3] Moreover, I came to understand that "the one who sent me is with me" (John 8:29a)! With Jesus of Nazareth, who redeemed me and gave me this opportunity, I now live only by this presence (by the Spirit) that abides within!

Emergency Preparedness: Model for Ministry

The worst danger to the survival of a people is the failure to have a change of heart with regard to respect for one another. The essence of this statement was the central idea of a prophetic announcement

---

3. Grace and faith are both a gift and virtue of God.

Ministry Focus

and revelational discourse in an interview in June 1998 with James S. Gilmore III, then governor of the Commonwealth of Virginia, regarding terrorism or a terrorist attack on the United States of America. Too often arrogant dispositions and selfish attitudes continue to make for war and violence. These ills of society underpin and make necessary an emergency preparedness plan as part of the continuing concern and mission of the church.

Lack of Preparedness for Emergencies

Early on in the project I engaged in conversation with Reverend Ben Campbell, pastoral director of Richmond Hill Ecumenical Christian Center. He pointed out several statistics involving the churches that centered on regional compartmentalization and denominational boundaries among or within various church associations, districts, and so forth. We also reviewed what churches are or should be doing collaboratively in community when it comes to disaster planning and support services for the affected or victimized population. We briefly reflected on the Hurricane Katrina (August 2005) experience in New Orleans and how the churches there might have been better able to assist the affected community had there been proper emergency plans in place. Of course we had no immediate answers.

The inability or unwillingness of some local churches to cooperate progressively in programs to benefit the broader community beyond the single church congregation is embarrassingly obvious and demonstrates a lack of stewardship in many black churches in both urban and rural settings. Churches are today confronted with and plagued by reduced attendance in membership, concomitant with dwindling resources for the overall maintenance or expansion of the physical structure, not to mention desired and necessary support of salaried professionals and program growth. Local church leadership officials in many cases are finding it increasingly more urgent to keep salaries paid in lieu of outreach ministries. Recognition of the alarming need to address grave economic, political, and social issues as well as a seemingly

Crisis and Emergency Management and Preparedness

unending list of various disasters and threats with courageous and proactive leadership could mitigate if not resolve or reverse these awful scourges on society, especially within the African American community. The results of a unified base of dedicated and faithful community leaders and resource providers could be astronomical and begin precipitously to blossom and/or establish expansive outreach human support ministries and provide improved or needed home-based support to growing ranks of youth and the senior population. The conditions of social existence—especially homelessness, adult and youth illiteracy, venereal disease, unemployment, violent crime, drug abuse, and so forth—in some urban centers and even in rural areas demand no less than full and unselfish cooperation by pastoral leaders throughout the faith community. Using models of success from other sectors or venues within the bounds of Christian faith and practice should yield a workable emergency preparedness plan.

Within the context of my overall ministry, I believe Christians everywhere should take the mission of emergency management and preparedness very seriously. When practical and proactive steps are taken toward effective emergency management and preparedness, I believe that many of the social ills identified above will be mitigated or solved. M. Scott Peck, in *The Road Less Traveled and Beyond*, observes, "We are all Israel; (that) there are today three meanings to the word 'Israel.' One refers to a rather small area of the earth's surface on the eastern coast of the Mediterranean. A second refers to the Jewish people, dispersed the world over. But the most basic meaning refers to the people who have struggled with God."[4] According to Peck, Christians are challenged to see an Israel that includes the entirety of our struggling infant humanity. Failure to follow this paradigm of theological enlightenment and reflection, coupled with appropriate civil preparedness, will doom the church and the world in the ever-widening destructive forces of natural and other human-caused disasters generated primarily by discordant and divisive human behavior.[5]

4. Peck, *Road Less Traveled and Beyond*, 250.
5. Ibid, 249–50.

Ministry Focus

Theodicy Visited

Though not central to this project—rather a motivating force in thinking about the nature of God and of creation, science, and evil—I will delve into this notion to give the reader an insight into my musings on acts of God and natural disasters per se. First, causality or guilt may be defined in any number of ways, depending on the social location of the interpreter. If a presupposition is made that disasters are the result of some evil or injustice against the divine, it may be explained by indicating or pointing to the occurrence as a function of theodicy, that is, to characterize the "disaster as being the will of God rather than a meaningless happening, and that gave a reason for including the denunciation of oppressors and pronouncements of judgment against them, provided they were part of a structure which included warning for the present and hope for the future."[6] Still, in case doubt or suspicion remains regarding the existence or genesis of disasters, it makes expedient and good sense that emergency management and preparedness be appropriated and embraced consistent with the purpose of God working in and through the various ambiguities of human activity. A scholar commenting on the text of Jeremiah (see Chapter 3) suggests that:

> the prophet adopts a horror rhetoric that reveals the dangerous aspects of the relationship between God and Israel and communicates to his audience its potential for horror and destruction. Elsewhere in Jeremiah, the prophet adopts a different destructive, violent rhetoric and assures his audience that there is also the potential for love and intimacy in Israel's relationship with God (Jeremiah 31). The rhetoric of horror in the book of Jeremiah describes a relationship between God and Israel, but does so in an effort to convince its readers to reform their ways in order to foster a constructive, intimate relationship with God.[7]

---

6. Houston, *Contending for Justice*, 74.

7. Kalmanofsky, *Horrors, Monsters, and Theology in the Book of Jeremiah*, 142. The author references Renita J. Weems's *Battered Love*, who notes, "the

Crisis and Emergency Management and Preparedness

Sociological Perspective

What does the church have to do with emergency management and preparedness? Is not this subject best left with crisis and consequence management planners, professionals, and operational response and recovery specialists at the federal, state, and local government levels? However, I, being a career servant and a veteran emergency management professional who is also an ordained pastor and minister of the gospel of Jesus Christ, believe that churches must also be concerned about and involved in emergency management and preparedness as an extension of ministry. The writer of 2 Corinthians 5:11–21 exhorts believers to undertake the ministry of reconciliation, that "God, who reconciled us to Himself through Christ and gave us the ministry of reconciliation: that God was reconciling the world to Himself in Christ, not counting men's sins against them. And He has committed to us the message of reconciliation. We are therefore Christ's ambassadors, as though God was making His appeal through us. We implore you on Christ's behalf: Be reconciled to God."

Paul Minear suggests that, upon hearing the voice of God, man's first inclination is usually to run. To undergird this suggestion, he cites Psalm 139:7:

> Whither shall I go from thy Spirit?
> Or whither shall I flee from thy presence?

Minear writes, "in a sermon on this psalm, Paul Tillich has described how we hate the Companion who is always present, how we resent the Knowing One from whom no secret is hid, how we try to escape from Him who is always interfering with our plans."[8] He states:

> it is from the arena (of divine visitation) that prophets and apostles speak. Each of them has tried to find an escape route, but has come to the blank wall of Job: 'He shutteth up a man, and there can be no opening'

God who loves and rescues is the same God who destroys and abandons" (7–8).

8. Minear, *Eyes of Faith*, 16–17.

Ministry Focus

(Job 12:14). Henceforth man speaks as a wrestler with God. The prophet resents God's intrusion, and yet his resentment is overborne. The psalmist struggles with immediate danger, convinced that the outcome of his conversation with God is a matter of life or death. The historian tells his story in an emergency to mobilize the memory of the community for the crucial choice.[9]

A sage of old recorded a remarkable if not mysterious observation: "The heavens are telling the glory of God; and the firmament proclaims His handiwork. Day to day pours forth speech, and night to night declares knowledge. There is no speech, nor are there words; their voice is not heard; yet their voice goes out through all the earth, and their words to the end of the world" (Ps 19:1–4a). Some learned scholars and scientists have inferred that there are mixed messages in our cosmic and earthly existence. Closer to the truth, however, is that the natural world is not merciless, offering horrible spectacles of terror and suffering as some have stated. Catastrophes such as storms, floods, and earthquakes claim thousands of innocent lives, and scores of terrible diseases spread death and despair. The heavens are telling, but are we listening? This is the voice or word I think was given to the prophet Elijah while on the mountain, as written in 1 Kings 19:11–13. There were many disastrous effects occurring in Elijah's environment; however, he not only had to observe the four occurrences, but he also was challenged to listen before proper preparations could be made for his next assignment.

How one acts or practices his or her faith often communicates or reveals one's actual motivation and personality. It's been said that "one has to understand his motivations to begin with, and especially the most human of human motivations, which is man's search for meaning—Meaning must be found and cannot be given. And it must be found by oneself, by one's own conscience."[10] Existentially, this may be observed in one's vocational commitments, passion, recreational pursuits, or worship tradition. In

9. Ibid., 19.
10. Frankl, *Man's Search*, 105.

other words, certain personal attributes and theological perspectives are modeled in outward or "creative action" (ortho-praxis) where theory informs the action.[11] Within the context of Maslow's *Motivation and Personality*, this characteristic trait has markedly influenced, motivated, and shaped my ministry. Reflective rationality and natural-societal phenomena have been the determining anchors and foundations upon which I've approached assignments and tasks, argued the essence of reality, and accomplished missions during this lowly and sometimes lonely pilgrimage.[12] One writer has noted, "when God invades man's consciousness, man's reliance on 'peace and security' vanishes from every nook of his existence. His life as a single whole becomes vulnerable. Broken down are the bulkheads between the chambers which confine explosions to one compartment. When God chooses man, (H)e invests him with full responsibility for total obedience to an absolute demand."[13]

It is not always, if ever, unquestionably clear why one acts or thinks in the way one does. However, this much is true: to practice servant leadership, one must gain or have personal or inner peace. What this means is that a healthy servant-leadership style emanates from a healthy lifestyle. In other words, one must become intimate with her or himself through introspection and continuous self-examination. This requires an action plan. It is suggested that one who desires to practice a Christian leadership style start with the Bible and structure the plan of action around God's Word. Find selected scriptures that speak to the condition that one finds inescapable and rehearse them over and over until they become consciously and subconsciously embedded. This is similar to a condition referred to in the Indian Vedas:

---

11. Musser and Price, *Handbook of Christian Theology*, 401–2. According to Musser, et al., a "praxis theology is the critical reflection or an action, in the light of faith commitment, that grows out of and seeks to contribute to the transformation of a social order, the creation of a new way of being the church, and the cultivation of a spirituality that is historically committed in the world. It is a form of reflection on the struggles by which the oppressed attempt to satisfy their innermost needs."

12. Maslow, *Motivation and Personality*, 22.

13. Minear, *Eyes of Faith*, 115.

Ministry Focus

"That which does the seeing, cannot be seen; that which does the hearing, cannot be heard; and that which does the thinking, cannot be thought."[14]

Offering a script for a way toward transformed thinking, teaching, and responsibility, Parker Palmer often quotes the words of Abba Felix when he makes such statements as, "There are no more words nowadays. When the brothers used to consult the old men and when they did what was said to them, God showed them how to speak. But now, since they ask without doing that which they hear, God has withdrawn the grace of the word from the old men and they do not find anything to say, since there are no longer any who carry out their words."[15] Palmer offers a piece of personal advice when he notes that "words were taken from me because I failed to follow their leading." He says further, "Seldom do we live up to the truth we are given, but that does not mean we must cease speaking the truth. Instead, we must be obedient to the whole of our truth—including our frequent failure to live it out."[16] Palmer observes that instruction will be withheld if one does not heed the advice offered.

One's moral salvation is the reward of keeping faith with the inner voice of nature. Charles Taylor insists, "Our moral salvation comes from recovering authentic moral contact with ourselves."[17] Authenticity of self is a way of living that engages or seeks a heroic dimension to life, with a sense of higher purpose, of something worth dying for. It aspires to abundant life with passion, embraces one's past as abundantly relevant, accepts the demands of citizenship, encourages and supports the duties of community solidarity, and promotes actions to satisfy the needs of the natural environment. In effect, "ideal authenticity" is an individual expression of what a better and higher mode of life would be, where "better" and

---

14. Quoted in Frankl, *Man's Search*, 37.
15. Palmer, *To Know as We Are Known*, 106.
16. Ibid.
17. Taylor, *Ethics of Authenticity*, 27.

"higher" are defined not in terms of what we happen to desire or need, but in terms of a standard of what we ought to desire.[18]

In the final analysis, it appears that human behavior is a major contributor to the condition of the earth's natural order of being; negative human behavior inadvertently influences natural disasters. If this is so, as some have argued, emergency management and preparedness is not an option, and the church shares a moral obligation.

Context of the Target Group: Providence Park Baptist Church

Providence Park Baptist Church, established in 1876, is an urban church located within the city of Richmond, Virginia, in the north-side community of Providence Park, near the boundary of Henrico County. Providence Park Baptist Church is served and supported by some thirty-six ministries. For the 2009 church year, the congregation consisted of some five hundred members. Church highlights and other ministerial information may be found on the church's website (www.providencepark.org).

As noted and further explained in its constitution, the purpose of Providence Park Baptist Church is to promote the advancement of the kingdom of God as set forth in the Holy Bible and taught by Jesus of Nazareth. According to the Constitution of the church, it shall attain this end through the maintenance of public worship of God and preaching of the gospel, consistent with Christian living by its members, personal evangelism, missionary endeavor, and Christian education.

In April 2004, the Providence Park Baptist Church Coordinating Survey Planning Team developed a survey instrument for the purpose to identify areas of strengths and weakness in its ministries.[19] The effort had as its primary goal to improve the efficiency and effectiveness of the church ministries. It was decided

18. Ibid., 27–29.
19. Providence Park Baptist Church, "Results of Congregational Survey."

Ministry Focus

that a survey research procedure would be the most effective tool to gather the necessary data.

The survey instrument included forty-seven items composing eight sections: demographics, discipleship, evangelism, facility services, fellowship, member services, ministry, worship, and leadership, and a comments section. An opportunity to complete the survey was given to all approximately 250 active members, consisting of various ministries of the church, including the congregation at large. With 132 people completing the survey and a response rate of 53 percent, the church determined that the sample size provided an excellent description of the PPBC congregation.

The area that claimed our attention for the purpose of the PPBC Emergency Preparedness Plan project focused on the demographics aspect of the survey. Based on the results of the April 2004 survey, it was found that the Providence Park Baptist Church is a very maturing congregation (74 percent of respondents were over forty-five years of age). Half of the PPBC respondents (60 percent) are over fifty-five years of age. The age distribution showed that PPBC has many retired members. Thus, as outlined and developed in chapter 5, the two key areas of the project, (1) evacuation plan development and (2) health and medical services ministry, were prioritized as being the two foremost areas of interest from among other emergency planning concerns. The PPBC Emergency Plan would be designed to address primarily the demographics of the congregation, and specifically the maturing and aged population, to provide critical care and support to this segment of the PPBC community in the event of an emergency on site.

2

The State of the Art of This Model for Ministry

A Preparedness Posture

IN THIS CHAPTER I will examine the state of the art of this model for ministry, that is, to what extent an emergency preparedness posture will foster a more holistic approach for dealing with a myriad array of community needs and problems, which is now suggested by some members of the clergy and laity to be an overwhelming concern for several churches. One writer has compared the weavings of a person's life to a system of connecting dots. It is thus through the process of connecting the dots that have made an indelible impression on my life that has led perceptively to this ministry. Perhaps it is my heritage, underscored by unique challenges and opportunities that have coalesced, that urges me to address the subject of crisis and emergency management and preparedness for the African American church community.

From connecting the dots to challenging everything, the primary purpose of introspective and reflective searching and thinking is to inspire the initiated to discover or rediscover, among other things, "what it means to be African." In his book *Seeking the Sakhu*, Wade Nobles offers the African community a matrix or network—thoughts and expositions—consisting of psychological resources—tools to rescue, reclaim, and reconstruct one's birthright—designed to aid in the implementation or rebuilding of bridges that had been for years left unattended and ruined because of the acceptance and domination of artificial philosophical factors inadvertent or unintentionally adopted and practiced congruent with Westernized thinking. This notion suggests that the writer must shed and replace his or her thinking with the mindset that subscribes to the field of African or black psychology.[1] "Sakhu," a kemetic term adapted from other sources and expressed by the author, means "understanding, the illuminator, the eye, the soul of being, that which inspires."[2] Taken further, "Sakhu" means an action or disposition that permits or persuades one to acknowledge and embrace that "each of us comes from heaven and enters into the world to follow a special path and to fulfill a particular purpose."[3]

The Church's Identity

Through personal belief and self-understanding, there is a hope that can and must be expressed with believing faith—a faith that is first courageous and then plausible—so that some of the problems noticed in the ministerial context may be addressed collaboratively, strategically, and systematically. It goes almost without saying that key to building community are personal and professional credibility, ethics, integrity, knowledge, and relational skills. One writer notes, "if you want people to have faith and belief in God, you cannot rely on preaching along the lines of a particular church but must, in the first place, portray your God believably—and you

---

1. Nobles, *Seeking the Sakhu*, xxv.
2. Ibid.
3. Ibid. "Sakhu" in essence is the "knowing of oneself," and in mentality and praxis is an action or disposition that permits or persuades one to acknowledge and embrace the fact that we are individually and uniquely created for a preordained and special purpose. The challenge is to search until you find it. Nobles continues, "Basic to our awakening or becoming conscious of our own consciousness is a clear recognition of the process of 'thinking deeply' to discover self-realization" (xxvi, 62, 318, 337).

must act credibly yourself."[4] The community must also sense the need for action and change. You could say that "just as a small fire is extinguished by the storm while a large fire is enhanced by it—likewise a weak faith is weakened by predicaments and catastrophes, whereas a strong faith is strengthened by them."[5]

Friedrich Schleiermacher notes, "the general concept of 'Church,' if there is to be such a concept, must be derived principally from Ethics, since in every case the 'Church' is a society which originates only through human action and which can only through such continue to exist."[6] He writes further that the piety (i.e., devotion, fidelity) that forms the basis of all ecclesiastical communions ("church") is, considered purely in itself, neither a Knowing nor a Doing, but a modification of Feeling, or of immediate self-consciousness. Schleiermacher holds that it is only the maintenance, regulation, and advancement of piety that they (leaders of state or of science) should regard as the essential business of the church.[7] Moreover Schleiermacher remarks, "the Church can only persist and reach its perfection through that to which it owes its very existence; that is, all aspects of Christian life, is so far as they are based on the truth taught by the Spirit and contain features of Christ's likeness."[8]

The Church's Mission

The church (Christian community universal) can effect positive interactions among and within the human enterprise, i.e., its mission is to participate with the Divine Eternal in creating a new heaven and new earth. The church has many purposes, for instance, to worship God, nurture believers to maturity in faith, and be a ministry of mercy that includes caring for the poor and

4. Frankl, *Man's Search*, 18.
5. Ibid, 19.
6. Schleiermacher, *Christian Faith*, 3.
7. Ibid, 5, 6.
8. Ibid, 584–86.

The State of the Art of This Model for Ministry

needy in the name of the Lord.[9] The church has also been referred to as the body of Christ. That is,

> the embodiment model has been central to ecclesiology; it has been one of the ways that organic thinking has flourished in Christianity. The model has encouraged a sense of unity of Christians with one another in and across denominational lines as well as with Christ, the head of the body. It has also supported a sense of uniqueness and privilege within the Christian community: we are the body of the savior of the world.[10]

While the church generally as a community has done much to prepare and respond to disasters, a more proactive role by local churches in the African-American church community must be done. We must come together to develop an emergency preparedness and response plan. Crisis and emergency management and preparedness is consistent with Christian missions, stewardship, and outreach. In many respects the church is a sanctuary, and, as such, it is "a projection of the community's belief in—a divinely ruled order that will ultimately triumph over the chaos of suffering. It offers a bridge between the struggles of this world and the joys of the world to come."[11]

Alienation and estrangement are the bases for negation among the church community at large and the context of ministerial work. There is a contagious and divisive culture that seems to emerge from the human or individual level up through families to nations around the world. Because negative behavior emanates in the heart, the root cause and corrective must be applied first to the heart of humanity—and this is specifically the work of the church animated by Christian faith. Although establishing hope and galvanizing the community to moral social action is a daunting challenge for anyone acting alone, the problems facing community including and especially the church must be confronted by members of the clergy, pastors, church leaders, and laity along

---

9. Grudem, *Systematic Theology*, 867–69.
10. McFague, *Body of God*, 205.
11. Lischer, *Preacher King*, 17.

Crisis and Emergency Management and Preparedness

with other community, state, and national leaders with no less than unified hearts, hands, and voices. Marcus Borg, on defining the heart of Christianity and describing what it means to be a part of a church, writes,

> In my judgment, the single most important practice is to be part of a congregation that nourishes you even as it stretches you. But if you are not involved in any church or are part of one that leaves you hungry and unsatisfied, find one that nurtures and deepens your Christian journey. Find one that makes your heart glad, so that you can wake up on Sunday morning filled with the anticipation of the psalmist: "I was glad when they said unto me, 'Let us go to the house of the Lord.'" Choosing a church is not primarily about feeling good, of course, but church is meant to nourish us, not to make us angry or leave us bored. If your church gives you a headache, it may be time to change.[12]

Common ground and clear imperatives are essential and must be defined and agreed upon among church leaders with God-centered covenant faithfulness. In the past, and perhaps to some extent today, churches have taken their ministries very seriously in terms of outreach to the disenfranchised and disposed.[13] Lack of initiative in this area and failure to cooperate collaterally and uniformly in the enterprise of emergency management and preparedness along with other crucial services will be devastating to the future of the church—not just local church but the church as a whole.

The work of the church must have meaning and be a way of life. What has been at the core of this chapter is how Christians must by faith engage with one another in covenant faithfulness,

---

12. Borg, *Heart of Christianity*, 193–94.

13. In his book cited earlier, Dr. Mitchell notes that "the church became, for all intents and purposes, a reincarnation of the African extended-family community.... Churches and the communities were proud of their capacity to care for the aged, widowed, crippled, homeless, and destitute.... The pattern is alive and well even today in some African American communities." Mitchell, *Black Church Beginnings*, 166–68.

The State of the Art of This Model for Ministry

just as Jesus Christ has with the church, in order to be serious about emergency planning. Borg summarizes his work with the statement: "At the heart of Christianity is the way of the heart—a path that transforms us at the deepest level of our being. At the heart of Christianity is the heart of God—a passion for our transformation and the transformation of the world. At the heart of Christianity is participating in the passion of God."[14] Failure to be kind and just with one another, between nation and nation, and people and people, will be as James Baldwin concludes in the headline notes—hence the title of his book—*The Fire Next Time*.[15]

Anyone who considers him or herself a Christian with an interest in emergency management and preparedness should examine three related works by Rodney Stark[16] and explore what is it about Christianity that offers hope and measures for survival. The specific interest here is to observe how Christianity historically may have contributed to the survival of a people, and if there are lessons for contemporary life. In referring to the rise of Christianity in various regions of the world, Stark notes, "Christianity not only offered a far more attractive and accessible eternal life, but a remarkably improved life here and now: Christians lived longer, better, and more securely than did their pagan neighbors."[17]

The context and role of the church as a sanctuary for its surrounding community proves or reveals that it's high time for the church to become an active partner in the demanding and growing cultural phenomenon of emergency and disaster awareness and planning. Emergencies and disasters come in all types and these risks, be they actual or viewed as threats, have demonstrated that they have no respect for boundaries and do not distinguish between the sacred and secular. Jonathan M. Barton, General Minister of the Virginia Council of Churches, a leading proponent for preparedness and response among the broad church community and a leading representative on the Commonwealth of Virginia Emergency

---

14. Borg, *Heart of Christianity*, 225.
15. Baldwin, *Fire Next Time*, 127.
16. "The Rise of Christianity," and .
17. Rodney, *Discovering God*, 318.

Response Team, noted, "In reflection on the Katrina response it was the churches, mostly the historical mainline churches, that played a major role in the response and helped to compensate for some of the governmental breakdown during that event."[18] Another commentator noted, "contrary to popular emphasis on FEMA, help after disaster in the United States has a small head and a very long tail. Various units of government are at the head, but thousands of faith-based groups make up the long tail."[19]

Returning to the account in Stark and the varied reasons given for the rise of Christianity, it appears the greatest genesis or initiative for the growth was the ability of the Christian community to survive in times of disaster. Stark notes,

> nothing demonstrates these contrasts so vividly as the ways to which Christians and pagans responded when the plagues struck the empire, as they did in the year 165 and again in 251. The pagan response was panic and retreat. . . . But this was not the case for how the Christians responded. Neither wealthy Christians nor the clergy fled, but took part in efforts to nurse the sick, not only their own kind, but many pagans as well. The

---

18. Reverend Barton is one of the contributors to this project. For information regarding the Virginia Council of Churches and its role in emergency management and preparedness within the Commonwealth of Virginia, contact Virginia Council of Churches, Inc., 1214 West Graham Road, Richmond, VA 23220. Email: barton@vcc-net.org.

19. Marvin Olasky, Professor of Journalism at the University of Texas, editor-in-chief of *World*, and author, in an address entitled "Responding to Disaster: Being Thankful for the Days without Disaster," stated, "The tail after Katrina was made up of all sorts of folks, but given the composition of the U.S. and especially the Southeast, it's no surprise that the overwhelming majority were Christians. Some of the bigger organizations quantified their help. Nine thousand Southern Baptists from 41 states volunteered 120,000 days during which they served 10 million meals and pushed forward cleanup and recovery efforts. During those same two months the Salvation Army served nearly 5 million hot meals and over 6.5 million sandwiches, snacks and drinks. Much more cumulatively was done by many other church groups that made up the tail. Our World magazine reporters in city after city throughout southern Louisiana and Mississippi heard words like these from Ronnie Harris, mayor of Gretna: 'Church workers were the first volunteers on the ground. It is churches that made the difference in Hurricane Katrina recovery.'"

The State of the Art of This Model for Ministry

fact that large numbers of Christians survived did not go unnoticed, lending immense credibility to Christian "miracle-working."[20]

Disasters are deeply rooted theologically, and therefore is a spiritual problem. In a related work highlighting the ecological crisis, Lynn White in a 1967 article observed,

> The historical roots of our ecological crisis are to be found in Christian theology, particularly in the Western tradition which led to modern scientific developments marked with a contemptuous and arrogant attitude toward the material world. Christian theology bears, therefore, a historical responsibility for the evil of the environmental destruction and should undergo a profound metanoia (*meaning to change one's mind*, repentance) in order to undo the damage it has caused.[21]

One writer recognizing this problem states, "We must stress that it is not any fear of impending disasters that obliges us to assume such initiatives. Rather, it is the recognition of the harmony that should exist between our attitudes and actions on one hand, and the laws of nature that govern the universe, on the other hand."[22] Another author, Delbert Vonvolkenburg, notes, "Those of us that have not planned for as many contingencies as possible are gambling with disaster, and the stakes are way too high not to plan properly."[23]

---

20. Stark, *Discovering God*, 319–20. In *The Rise of Christianity*, Stark notes, "In 165, during the reign of Marcus Aurelius, a devastating epidemic [the Plague of Galen] swept through the Roman Empire. Some medical historians suspect that it was the first appearance of smallpox in the West. But whatever the actual disease, it was lethal. During the fifteen-year duration of the epidemic, from a quarter to a third of the empire's population died from it, including Marcus Aurelius. Then in 251 a new and equally devastating epidemic again swept the empire, hitting the rural areas as hard as the cities. This time it may have been measles. Both smallpox and measles can produce massive mortality rates when they strike a previously unexposed population" (73).

21. White, "Historical Roots of Our Ecologic Crisis," 1204.

22. Chryssavgis, *Cosmic Grace + Humble Prayer*, 282–83.

23. Vonvolkenburg, *Keep Me Safe, O God*, iv.

Crisis and Emergency Management and Preparedness

One of the distinguished professors at Samuel DeWitt Proctor School of Theology aptly puts the notion that there needs to be a great revival in and among the African peoples to rediscover and regain their community.[24] So much has been lost as a result of inattention and slothfulness. Any community or organization that hopes to survive must have laws, policies, and rules. There must be a set of guiding principles. People need direction, and they need to be shepherded in a caring and responsible manner. Survival is a matter of preparation.

Embodied Hope

Preparation requires initiative, a preparedness mindset, and a survival plan. Understand that

> survival is dependent on direction. However, survival cannot be the supreme value. Unless life points to something beyond itself, survival is pointless and meaningless.... For there is hope for mankind's survival only as long as people will arrive at the awareness of common denominators in axiological terms—that is to say, common denominators in what they feel makes their lives worth living. What is "unknowable" need not be unbelievable. In fact, where knowledge gives up, the torch is passed on to faith.[25]

This project would not do justice to the efforts of some churches and key leaders were we to overlook the story and success of two clergypersons who took it upon themselves to help in times of great crisis. This amounts to a testament of how the church responded to the yellow fever epidemic that severely affected the population in and around Philadelphia during 1793–94. The yellow fever epidemic that hit the region of Philadelphia nearly wiped out all life in that city and devastated the remaining population. Yet because of the courage and determination of the Rt. Rev. Richard Allen[26] and

---

24. Sanders, *Blowing The Trumpet in Open Court*, 183–86.
25. Frankl, *Man's Search*, 134–35, 146.
26. See Allen, *Life, Experience, and Gospel Labors*.

The State of the Art of This Model for Ministry

Absalom Jones, two Christian leaders in that city, many persons were comforted, rescued, and saved from this violent epidemic. Moreover, several persons, including the political leadership of the city of Philadelphia, were given hope by the valiant efforts and leadership of these two clergypersons.

In "A Narrative of the Proceedings of the Colored People During the Awful Calamity in Philadelphia, in the Year 1793; and a Refutation of Some Censures Thrown upon Them in Some Publications," Absalom Jones and Richard Allen corroborated to share the story how they nearly single-handedly worked tirelessly to help save hundreds, if not thousands more, from the dreaded death that left no individual or home unscathed. Although there are many interesting stories that reflect how Richard Allen came to prominence, and about the catalyst, genesis, and origin of the AME Church, the particular focus here is directed to how Richard Allen and Absalom Jones partnered to render aid and comfort in light of the yellow fever epidemic that wreaked disease and havoc in the city of Philadelphia. A personal account documents some of the heroic acts of bravery:

> Early in September [1793], a solicitation appeared in the public papers to the people of color to come forward and assist the distressed, perishing and neglected sick; with a kind of assurance, that people of our color were not liable to take the infection; upon which we and a few others met and consulted how to act on so truly alarming and melancholy an occasion. After some conversation, we found a freedom to go forth, confiding in Him who can preserve in the midst of a burning, fiery furnace. Sensible that it was our duty to do all the good we could to our suffering fellow mortals, we set out to see where we could be useful. We administered what relief we could. . . . The Lord was pleased to strengthen us and remove all fear from us, and disposed our hearts to be as useful as possible. In order to better regulate our conduct, we called on the mayor next day, to consult with him on how to proceed so as to be most useful. We then offered our services in the public papers, by advertising that we could remove the dead and procure nurses. Our services

were the production of real sensibility; we sought not fee nor reward, until the increase of the disorder rendered our labor so arduous, that we were not adequate to the service we had assumed. The mortality increasing rapidly, obliged us to call in the assistance of five hired men in the awful charge of interring the dead. It was very uncommon, at this time, to find any one that would go near, much more handle a sick or dead person.[27]

Allen writes:

> When the sickness became general, and several of the physicians died, and most of the survivors were exhausted by sickness or fatigue, that good man, Dr. [Benjamin] Rush, called us more immediately to attend upon the sick, knowing that we could both bleed. He told us that we could increase our utility by attending to his instructions, and accordingly directed us where to procure medicine duly prepared, with proper directions how to administer them, and at what stages of the disorder to bleed; and when we found ourselves incapable of judging what was proper to be done, to apply to him, and he would, if able, attend them himself, or send Edward Fisher, his pupil, which he often did; and Mr. Fisher manifested his humanity by an affectionate attention for their relief. This has been no small satisfaction to us; for we think that when a physician was not attainable, we have been the instruments in the hands of God, for saving the lives of some hundreds of our suffering fellow mortals.[28]

Another work confirming the story by Allen and documented in a PBS Online article stated:

> Philadelphia's yellow fever epidemic of 1793 was the largest in the history of the United States, claiming the lives of nearly 4000 people. In late summer, as the number of deaths began to climb, 20,000 citizens fled to the countryside, including George Washington, Thomas

27. Ibid., 48–50.
28. Ibid., 50.

Jefferson, and other members of the federal government (at that time headquartered in Philadelphia). At the urging of Benjamin Rush, the support of Philadelphia's free black community was enlisted by Absalom Jones, Richard Allen, and William Gray, a fruitseller who along with Allen and Jones had secured support to build the African Church the previous year. In an effort to prove themselves morally superior to those who reviled them, Philadelphia's black community put aside their resentment and dedicated themselves to working with the sick and dying in all capacities, including as nurses, cart drivers, and grave diggers. Despite Rush's belief that blacks could not contract the disease, 240 of them died of the fever. As the weather cooled, the disease subsided, and the deaths stopped. Then accusations began against the black citizens who had worked so hard to save the sick and dying. The attack was led by Mathew Carey, whose pamphlet attacked many in the black community. A response to the pamphlet was published by Richard Allen and Absalom Jones.[29]

Gayraud Wilmore adds an inspiring note as a point of reference and closure to this case study. He notes that Richard Allen "had a desire for a church that would combine secular relevance with deep spirituality in a context of simplicity and spontaneity. . . . Allen believed that a black community had to be organized to deal responsibly with its own problems as long as prejudice and the lack of compassion refused to erase the color line."[30] May the churches of the twenty-first century learn a valuable lesson from the efforts of the Rt. Reverend Richard Allen and Absalom Jones, two great pioneers of the progressive African American Church movement in America who singularly took a stand and practiced emergency management and preparedness in the face of imposing odds during a catastrophic event.

The following is a testimonial given by Matthew Clarkson, mayor of Philadelphia, January 23, 1794, in recognition and

29. "Yellow Fever epidemic."
30. Wilmore, *Black Religion and Black Radicalism*, 105, 123.

Crisis and Emergency Management and Preparedness

commendation for services rendered to the people of Philadelphia during the yellow fever epidemic of 1793–94:

> Having, during the prevalence of the late malignant disorder, had almost daily opportunities of seeing the conduct of Absalom Jones and Richard Allen, and the people employed by them to bury the dead: I with cheerfulness give this testimony of my approbation of their proceedings, so far as they came under my notice. Their diligence, attention and decency of deportment, afforded me, at the time, much satisfaction.[31]

Richard Allen posts this final note of caution and encouragement for Christians and others everywhere who seek to prepare for and offer assistance to others during a time of a crisis or an emergency:

> We shall now conclude with the following proverb, which we think applicable to those of our color, who exposed their lives in the late afflicting dispensation:
>
> > "God and a soldier all men adore
> > In time of war and not before;
> > When the war is over, and all things righted,
> > God is forgotten, and the soldier slighted."[32]

In an article published in *The Richmond Voice* titled "Black Churches See a Revival of Community Cooperation," several members of the clergy on the national front pointed to a need to intensify efforts in addressing various ills that affect the black community. The article focused attention on there having been a "resurgence of interdenominational relations in some of the nation's most prominent Black churches" to seek ways to make a positive difference with risk populations. It was noted further that "while some are responding to the tragedy in Haiti and others are trying to revive the long-term efforts to help Black communities, they all

---

31. Allen, *Life, Experience*, 66.
32. Ibid., 65.

The State of the Art of This Model for Ministry

say they have determined they can do more together than any one group could do by itself."[33]

We are becoming much more aware of the need as well as the opportunity to be proactive within the local community, which includes local churches. While leadership is one of the foundational aspects of crisis and emergency management and preparedness, it is also important to note that "you don't have to be the lead, you don't have to be sitting behind a desk—sometimes the best service rendered is when you can work one-on-one with people to give them encouragement and hope."[34] During her interview with a disaster assistance employee with the Federal Emergency Management Agency, Elaine Pittman was made aware that "we need to look at the grass-roots organizations because those persons from vulnerable populations do have barriers—some of it could be a disability in terms of preparing for, responding to, recovering from, and mitigating and preventing disasters."[35]

As noted elsewhere in this project document, the context and role of the church proves or reveals that it's high time for the church to become a key partner in the demanding and growing cultural phenomenon of emergency and disaster awareness and planning. The saving grace is that the different preparedness and response plans on the local level can be tied together with the emergency plan for the church to embrace an underlying Christian perspective about why this ministry is important.[36]

In an eye-opening work titled *Introducing Black Theology of Liberation*, Dwight Hopkins indicates that a method must be observed and employed to capture the spirit or rhythm of cooperation within the African American community. "Method," he notes, "as a construction of a black theology of liberation, enables the African American church to carry out what God has called the church to believe in, preach, and do in this world. Method entails identifying the sources where God is already present . . . and

---

33. "Black Churches See a Revival of Community Cooperation," 8.
34. Pittman, "Spirit for Service," 25–27.
35. Ibid.
36. Kim, *Hope, Help, Heal*, 8.

Crisis and Emergency Management and Preparedness

working in solidarity with the least in society because that is where the divine can already be found."[37]

A piece of information obtained one week prior to the devastating earthquake that occurred on January 12, 2010, ravaging the Republic of Haiti, appears to be of value in supporting some of the underlying assumptions given or implied in this project. As reported in *The Richmond Voice*, and following a recent study on the effects of disasters on predominantly African American communities, documentation revealed that "people most likely to be affected by catastrophe tend to be the poorer persons who are either Black or other racial minorities.... Data were conclusive; the people most likely to be affected by catastrophe in the regions ... studied were disproportionately minorities, poor and living in housing that are substantially below regional and national average."[38] Other reports and related sources undergird the proposition that the African American church has essentially a moral authority to begin, and if begun, to continue to develop emergency plans and programs to assist the resident community and neighbors beyond the immediate borders of the local church.[39]

---

37. Hopkins, *Introducing Black Theology of Liberation*, 185.

38. "Demographics of Catastrophe," 21. According to *The Richmond Voice*, the study identified as "The Demographics of Catastrophe" was conducted by Peter J. McDonough, an adjunct professor at the Eagleton Institute of Politics, Rutgers University, and commissioned by ProtectingAamerica.org. The study, reportedly released October 2009, "compared the statewide demographic profile of persons living in Louisiana, Mississippi, Florida and Texas with that of the U.S. population generally."

39. In a work titled *Rediscovering Black Conservatism*, Lee H. Walker, Senior Fellow at the Heartland Institute, cites several stories throughout the book that speak to accountability and responsibility by people and communities in high-risk areas from various kinds of types of emergencies. Lee notes, "In his 1967 book, *The Crisis of the Negro Intellectual*, Harold Cruse contended that the American left of the 1950s did more harm than good to the politics and the culture of black America. The left helped create a culture of dependence, entitlement, and victimization amongst a formerly resilient people who had taken immense steps forward during the preceding decades. Unfortunately, the ideologies of the American left are still alive among many groups of blacks today" (63).

The State of the Art of This Model for Ministry

One of the keys to successful emergency planning within the context of the local church is to identify persons who will volunteer their services and commit to the overall preparedness, response, and recovery parameters of a crisis or emergency environment. Because it is quite unlikely—perhaps even impractical—for the local government to have sufficient personnel to respond to every emergency situation in a timely fashion, church leaders and community volunteers must come forward and avail themselves of training opportunities, emergency coordination, leadership skills development, and other aspects of crisis and emergency preparedness. In most congregations there are persons with requisite skills as a result of prior military service and training, retired first responders, paramedical experience, and so forth. These combined assets can become a critical and vast army of church and community support when properly trained and coordinated.

Someone once noted that there is an enemy that would thwart the combined and well-meaning efforts of many to do the right thing. Moreover, we have been warned to be on the lookout and defensive for the evil one lurking in our midst, whose strategy is to destroy or overturn progress to build and maintain community by many who are considered our trailblazers. C. S. Lewis, in his classic book *The Screwtape Letters*, ironically and satirically portrays Screwtape as the villainous senior official of the underworld, and Wormwood, his protégé, whose purpose in life is to distort reality and destroy the created divine order. What Lewis describes "as the technique of 'diabolical ventriloquism' is indeed still there: Screwtape's whites are our blacks and whatever he welcomes we

---

In his book titled *Survival: How a Culture of Preparedness Can Save You and Your Family from Disasters*, Lt. Gen. Russell L. Honoré (U.S. Army, Ret.) enlarges on some of the same themes noted in Lee's book. *Survival* reveals some of the issues that are associated with a people who have become inattentive to the context of their existence. From firsthand experiences, General Honoré notes, "some of that failure to act is a function of a too-busy society overwhelmed by other problems and unwilling to take the time necessary to attend to the details of preparedness. But some of it is a function of believing that the government will step in and make things right when they go wrong. As we saw in Katrina, the government is not always in a position to do that as quickly or as efficiently as we think it will" (219-20).

should dread."[40] In case of doubt, Lewis extends a word of caution: "Readers are advised to remember that the devil is a liar."[41] Sound familiar? In his memoirs Martin Luther comments that "he never had any conflicts of any kind within, which he did not attribute to the personal agency of the devil."[42]

Perhaps it is the invisible nature of the church that gets us into so much trouble when it comes to developing and keeping community and cooperation. Sometimes it's easy to get lost in the building, that is, the "church"—its architecture, grounds, and instruments, and with questions involving the budget or justification for use of funds, and so forth. Jargon infiltrates the assembly, undermines faith, and impedes consistency in decision making. This further erodes community and often results in confusion, disappointment, and thus failure to follow through on crucial goals, objectives, and associated tasks. This is, too, the nature of "failed" emergency planning. Disaster preparedness is a business and requires teamwork. Susan Kim noted, "It is complex. It involves federal, state and local governments, voluntary agencies, insurance companies, the military, and many, many others. But it is also a theology. It involves churches and their people—being involved requires statement of faith on the part of church leaders."[43]

40. Lewis, *Screwtape Letters with Screwtape Proposes a Toast*, 180.

41. Ibid., ix. There is a scripture that might lend truth to this statement: "You belong to your father, the devil, and you want to carry out your father's desire. He was a murderer from the beginning, not holding to the truth, for there is no truth in him. When he lies, he speaks his native language, for he is a liar and the father of lies" (John 8:44 NIV).

42. Hazlitt, *Table Talk of Martin Luther*, lxxxvi. The translator/editor notes, "On this subject the following expressions are recorded of Luther: — 'When the devil comes to me in the night, I give him these and the like answers: — 'Devil! I must now sleep, for the command and ordinance of God is, that we should labor by day, and sleep by night.' Then, if he goes on with the old story, and accuses me with being a sinner, I say to him, '*Holy Satan, pray for me!*' or else, '*Physician, heal thyself!*' 'The best way to drive out the devil, if he will not go for texts of Scripture, is to jeer and flout him, for he cannot bear scorn'" Emphasis original.

43. Kim, *Hope, Help, Heal*, 10.

The State of the Art of This Model for Ministry

Throughout this endeavor and the ensuing search and review of works related to the project, I found scant if any applications or in-depth details of emergency preparedness for churches. What plans that were discovered provided little help in the way of examples or practical steps of how to go about or engage the business of emergency preparedness in the sense that were undertaken in this project. As may be examined and utilized, the planning format offered in this project document presents a rather straightforward, field-tested model that would aid a local church in the development of an emergency plan for the church and its community. As noted in the outset of this project, there is evidently a dearth of essential information to satisfy a growing problem in communities that are at greatest risk of perishing in time of a crisis or catastrophe. This requirement must be met with a model that offers a practical means to satisfy a critical need. This document offers a guide and tool that faith communities may employ in the area of emergency preparedness. Moreover, this document is designed to add to the body of knowledge that may help protect and save lives in the event of a natural or human-caused disaster or emergency.

3

Theoretical Foundations for the Model

Methodology for Finding Safety in the Sanctuary

> ¹¹For surely I know the plans I have for you, says the LORD, plans for your welfare and not for harm, to give you a future with hope. ¹²Then when you call upon me and come and pray to me, I will hear you. (Jer 29:11–12)

Exegetic Composition

IN A LETTER TO an exiled people, Jeremiah elicits a paradox of divine activity (29:11, 12b) urging a faithful response (29:12a) on the part of the respective audience (2:2–4) to be reinstated after a season (29:10) of divinely appointed correctives (36:2–3) and be restored to covenanted promises (30:3) formerly forfeited by unfaithfulness (1:16). Historically, 29:11–12 forms the centerpiece or focal point in a passage (29:1–32) that deals with instructions to a people who are besieged (under exile), on the one hand, and commending their confidence and consolation to be obedient to the directive, on the other, with the end result being the sustainment of life. By way of analogy, the Jeremiah text is central to the project and frames this author's motivations. The message is that the church's welfare is based on performance that is consistent with the emergency plan.

From the perspective of divine activity as here prophesied by Jeremiah, the messenger of God literally testifies that while there will be suffering for a season, hope, though conditional, is assured and the people will be restored. The success of the plan that projects a future and hope for a people in the face of disaster is predicated upon rightful action based on information communicated to the community by the messenger.

In terms of form, structure, and movement, this pericope, contained as it is within a larger biblical context, provides an announcement of judgment that is juxtaposed or offset by a prediction of salvation. The announcement is given at a time in Judah's history when the nation is hopeful they would be able to resist or successfully rebel against Babylonian domination. Moreover, while the nation Judah may view the prophetic statement (29:11) as inconsistent or unjustified based on nationalistic ambitions, it is nevertheless linked to the backdrop of Judah's apostasy and broken covenant relationship (28:1–4). Further, the nation may not have realized that it was the divine plan of the Lord to bring the people to repentance (36:2–3) through the temporary suffering of being exiled. Jeremiah was called (1:10) to give instructions for this divine purpose and to urge the people to faithfully accept and fulfill the conditions of the proposition (29:12a).

I am compelled to share the message with the African American church community that they must participate in emergency preparedness programs and have an emergency plan to save lives and protect property. Crisis and emergency management and preparedness is a mission that many state and local governments, along with the federal government, take very seriously. Providence Park Baptist Church has been selected as the target community for this project, and we of that church will jointly endeavor to complete the task consistent with the intended goal and end results.

The theological perspective for this work is precipitated through the lens of the Old Testament prophet Jeremiah. It is noted that "Ancient as well as current beliefs about Yahweh and his

Crisis and Emergency Management and Preparedness

covenant people are refracted through the man Jeremiah, to which are added numerous witnesses to the life of faith which grows out of Jeremiah's own prophetic experience."[1]

The text of the epigraph above suggests that, while both wars and other forms of disaster are indicators of divine action—though not necessarily of a broken relationship with the creator of the universe—they may occur to demonstrate the sovereignty of God. This means that whether there be war or disaster, destruction or loss of home or property, or other calamities, our confidence and hope is to be in God. We can endure and live with and through disasters, knowing that our condition and context offers hope and promises restoration in the final analysis.

These verses point to a Jeremiah who knew "a God who 'knows.' He knows people and he knows events, not only those events which are current but also those planned for the future."[2] Furthermore,

> Jeremiah realized that Yahweh punishes entire cities for unrighteous living (5:1–8), and that a point can be reached where mediation for such cities is no longer possible (7:16–20; 11:14–17; 14:11–12; 15:1–2). Not only immoral prophets, but also seemingly innocent people, such as the man who brought the news of Jeremiah's birth to his father, are likened by Jeremiah to the inhabitants of these proverbial cities (20:15–16; 23:14) and must suffer a like fate when Jerusalem is destroyed.[3]

Jeremiah was called and committed to his mission. His entire lifestyle as recorded in Scripture puts him on a course to communicate as well as complete a charge given to him at an earlier age by divine revelation. Jeremiah left no directive unfulfilled as internalized in his consciousness. He left no love unshared with those he knew God loved, and Jeremiah did not allow personal defeat or humiliation to prevent him from conveying the words of life. The challenge of effective communication sometimes occasions one to

---

1. Freedman, *Anchor Bible Dictionary*, vol. 3, 716.
2. Ibid., 717.
3. Ibid.

resort to methods or techniques to excite the senses of the listener or observer so as to cause or encourage desired action.

Contextually, the work of the messenger or communicator is often made difficult when the audience is unable or unwilling to see the future—regardless how bleak or hopeful—because of preoccupation with present conditions. In a similar vein, it may be difficult for one to come to understand that their present circumstance is partly or primarily the byproduct of a failure to learn from previous experiences, and somehow even going so far as to dismiss past practices as not being relevant. Another condition that accompanies the incapacity to discern or realize a distant future is a lack of awareness or appreciation of future consequences. A messenger who is gifted, however, by virtue of practice or profession in a particular field may have the advantage and be extremely influential in helping others to see the larger picture of a future possibility, potential, or prospect.

It bears repeating that security—personal, community, national or otherwise—begins within the heart, soul, and mind of the individual. The concern for security is driven by the desire for peace. As interestingly as it may appear from the Jeremiah sayings, "both judgment and hope are held together" by the peace of God for people who might be struggling to understand their plight, especially for persons seeking to hold fast to their Christian faith.[4] In connection with this line of reasoning, Walter Brueggemann notes that people who may be going through the valley of the shadow of death experiences "must find ways to live faithfully and hopefully" in the midst of despair.[5] Brueggemann characterizes Jeremiah as "practicing pastoral care among the exiles. That pastoral care is expressed around two convictions: (a) there must be a realistic and intentional *embrace of the Exile* as a place where Jews must now be and where God has summoned them to obedience (29:5–7), and (b) there is *a long-term hope for return and restoration* that can be affirmed and accepted (vv. 10–14). . . . The Exile is a place where God's faithful promises work a profound newness."[6]

4. *New Interpreter's Bible*, vol. 6, 792.
5. Brueggemann, *To Build, to Plant*, 29.
6. Ibid., 30. Emphasis original.

Reflectively and summarily therefore, we discover evil is present in the world and is manifested by human behavior. To argue or posit that disasters are the result of the presence of evil in human relationships is to knowingly make an extreme presupposition some would say is blatantly unfounded. However, on close reading of several sources related to Jeremiah's journal, and especially those that appear to explore or seek to uncover his theology, "Jeremiah has been faithful to his prophetic vocation as 'prophet to the nations' with the agenda that he must 'pluck up and tear down' (Jeremiah 1:10). This dismantling of Jerusalem and then of Babylon has been accomplished in poetic discourse by a rich complex of images, including the *rejection of infidelity, the invasion of war, terminal illness*, and *foolishness that leads to death*. All of these images serve as rhetorical strategies for divine judgment."[7] But that was only one dimension of Jeremiah's mission; he had a "mandate to 'plant and build—a mandate enacted in performative speech that is promise-laden.... Thus, two pairs of verbs in the prophetic call of 1:10 are programmatically sequenced in 31:28:

> And just as I have watched over them to pluck up and break down, to overthrow, destroy, and bring evil, so I will watch over them *to build* and *to plant*, says the Lord. (Jer 31:28)

The God who 'watched over my work to perform it' (1:12), concerning destruction, is the God who will now watch to see that the work of 'plant and build' is fully enacted."[8]

Sibley Towner, in his book titled *How God Deals with Evil*, notes, "one understanding of how God deals with evil is what

---

7. Brueggeman, *Theology of the Book of Jeremiah*, 115. Emphasis original.

8. Ibid., 116. Emphasis original. Mignon R. Jacobs notes in his essay "Favor and Disfavor in Jeremiah 29:1–23": "In particular, Jeremiah 29 extends the perspectives of chapters 24–28 and depicts God's plan, including the wellbeing and *hopeful* future of God's favored people. Yet, the reassurance to this people is immediately juxtaposed to the planned demise of the disfavored others. It is no surprise, then, that some interpreters readily highlight the hopeful and minimize the promised demise of the disfavored. Even so, the conceptual framework of the text challenges any reconceptualization that ignores its characterization of the multiple dimensions of God's character" (131).

Theoretical Foundations for the Model

theologians call divine retribution."[9] Towner continues "the motif of divine retribution is a powerful one in all parts of the Old and New Testaments. It is one of the important themes by which the canonical writers sought to depict God's way of dealing with human autonomy and sin. Although it stands in relationship with—and even subordinate to—other Biblical themes, it has to be reckoned with seriously."[10] Towner suggests that "all the proximate cause-and-effect sequences, all the historical joys and tragedies, all the retributions, great and small, are framed by [God's] ultimate power to complete that purpose—i.e., that God's purpose in the world is to save it, all of it, from utter defacement and ultimate destruction and to preserve it, all of it, to be his joy and companion forever-to redeem the world."[11] He notes further,

> most of us want help, Biblical or otherwise, to enable us to see the way between the extremes of permissiveness on the one hand and punitive retribution on the other, whether the issue be our own personal behavior or our understanding of the way in which God deals with his creation. Biblical theology can perform a service of signal contemporary importance. It can reassemble the data bearing on the motif of divine retribution in order to sketch out a perspective on God's justice and love which will adequately take into account all sides of the Biblical witness to the theme.[12]

The Philosophy of Planning

The Christian community can influence positive interactions among and within the human enterprise, that is, its mission is to participate with the Divine Eternal in creating a new heaven and new earth. The thrust of this chapter is to offer the target community a planning paradigm upon which to build or renew its

9. Towner, *How God Deals with Evil*, 9.
10. Ibid., 11.
11. Ibid., 12–13.
12. Ibid., 22.

Crisis and Emergency Management and Preparedness

commitment to engage in faithful readiness in times of a disaster or emergency. The church—God/humanity dynamic—is the covenant-based centerpiece of our existence, founded on Jesus Christ, Son of the Living God, and the sole purpose of the function of the church in the world. Interreligious dialogue between churches must be intensified to include governmental and other professional organizations in the emergency preparedness process, and the initiation of discussion and action in the development of plans and procedures must align with God's intent (Jer 29:11) to guard against disasters. Hazard awareness and identification underscore the need for emergency management and preparedness and cannot be fully addressed outside the theological context. That was the intent of broadening the emergency preparedness team concept to include community or cooperative outreach ministries. The Cooperative Outreach Ministry (COM) as noted in this document consists of five churches: First Baptist Church, Washington Park; Good Hopewell Baptist Church, Florida Avenue; Providence Park Baptist Church, Providence Park; Seventh Street Baptist Church, Meadowbridge Road; and St. John Baptist Church, Washington Park.

Planning Model

In terms of planning objectives, Delbert Vonvolkenburg suggests the purpose of the planning process is threefold:[13] (1) to awaken, (2) encourage, and (3) equip the congregation for any contingency. He explains as follows:

- *To Awaken*: Ensure that the community is aware of the types of emergencies that are most likely to occur in the specific community.

- *To Encourage*: Assist each member of the congregation to identify and use their gifts and skills in such

---

13. Vonvolkenburg, *Keep Me Safe, O God*, iv. The Vonvolkenburg planning paradigm is the primary model employed for this project.

Theoretical Foundations for the Model

a manner that one will have something to contribute to the overall cause.

- *To Equip*: Using the emergency plan, persons who have the requisite professional background and talents may be called upon and tasked to offer consultation and training and to prepare individuals overall to react to an emergency should one occur. Training is to be continued through the years, and education should occur as new members and officers are added.

Vonvolkenburg writes that the congregation and leaders should be directed first to look at what types of emergencies have occurred in the community, and/or at the facility.[14] He puts these in the categories of historical, geographical, technological, human error, and physical.

Historical	Geographical	Technological	Human Error	Physical
• Fires	• Proximity to Flood Plain, Dams, etc.	• Fires or explosion	• Poor Training	• The Physical Construction of the Site
• Severe Weather	• Proximity to Companies That Produce or Store Hazardous Materials	• Safety System Failures	• Poor Maintenance	• Hazardous Processes or By-products
• Hazardous Materials Spills	• Proximity to Major Transportation Routes and Airports	• Telecommunications Failure	• Carelessness	• Facilities for Storing Combustibles

14. Ibid., 14–17.

Crisis and Emergency Management and Preparedness

Historical	Geo-graphical	Techno-logical	Human Error	Physical
• Transportation Accidents	• Proximity to Nuclear Power Plants	• Computer System Failure	• Misconduct	• Layout of Equipment
• Earthquakes		• Power Failure	• Substance Abuse	• Lighting
• Hurricanes		• Heating, Cooling System Failure	• Fatigue	• Evacuation Routes and Exits
• Tornadoes		• Emergency Notification System Failure		• Proximity to Shelter Areas
• Terrorism		• Water System Failure		
• Utility Outages				

Table 1. Hazard Categories and Components

In practice, emergency management planning elements include:

- Direction and Control
- Communications
- Life Safety
- Property Protection
- Community Outreach
- Recovery and Restoration
- Administration and Logistics

Theoretical Foundations for the Model

After the adoption or identification of planning elements, the following CEMP aspects should be considered and developed:

- Emergency response procedures
- Supporting documents
- Emergency training curriculum and schedule

The Emergency Planning Coordinator for Providence Park Baptist Church will use and present the supplied model plan template format. The presentation and discussions following during the planning session will outline the four critical steps in the CEMP Planning Process. Without exception they are:

- Establishment of a planning team
- Identification and analysis of capabilities and hazards
- Plan development
- Plan implementation

It has been explained that the four steps are valuable[15] because they help:

- Foster a safer environment for ministry;
- Reinforce the Scriptural basis for planning;
- Outline a broad approach to assembling a safety and security plan; and
- Articulate the multiple components or issues that need resolution to assembling such a plan including essential equipment and materials.

Planning Statement

The essence of the message to be presented to Providence Park Baptist Church at the outset of the emergency planning session will be

---

15. For further information on these steps, see Jacob Lewis Saylor's *Peace Be Still*, 10.

Crisis and Emergency Management and Preparedness

that Christians everywhere should take the mission of emergency management and preparedness very seriously. God chose Israel to be his witnesses, to be his servants, to be God's "treasured possession" (Isa 43:10; Exod 19:5–6). The New Testament writer of 1 Peter 2:9 lays this covenant commitment squarely on the shoulders of all believers in Jesus Christ, for we "are a chosen people, a royal priesthood, a holy nation, a people belonging to God that [we] may declare the praises of Him who called [us] out of darkness into His wonderful light." For the emergency preparedness team at Providence Park Baptist Church, this statement will be the undergirding planning focus and theme. Failure to follow this paradigm of theological enlightenment and reflection coupled with appropriate civil preparedness will doom the local as well as the larger church and the world to the ever-widening destructive forces of natural and other human-caused disasters generated primarily by discordant and divisive human behavior.

A. Planning Parameters

The assumption and understanding that a crisis or emergency can happen at any time and could affect one individual, single building or room, or the entire church facility will be emphasized. In addition, it will be stated that the emergency could be in close proximity to the church proper and thus require certain elements of the church plan to be implemented. Emergencies cause confusion and stress for all involved. To minimize these effects, initial activation and implementation of the church's emergency plan should always be handled in a calm, consistent manner. Efficient implementation of the plan will provide a clear direction, responsibility, and continuity of control for key officials, administrators, and the pastor. The basic idea to any well-constructed emergency plan is to minimize the possible threat to individuals and properties during an actual emergency.

Theoretical Foundations for the Model

B. Purpose

The purpose of the plan is to direct and provide actions intended to preserve life and protect property from further destruction in the event of an emergency. The overall plan establishes an emergency organization to direct and control operations during an emergency situation by assigning responsibilities to specific ministries and individuals. All essential ministries—trustees, diaconate, ushers, and particularly the health and medical support ministry—are to use any and all available resources when mitigating against, preparing for, responding to, and recovering from a natural or human-caused emergency.

In general, the plan will be structured to consist of the basic plan and appendices, and may include support or incident annexes for unique circumstances or hazards, and remote facility plans, for example, a church daycare facility, life center, or child development center. None of these may apply to Providence Park Baptist Church but will be noted as examples of activities or areas of concern. It will also be noted that the emergency plan should be sufficiently flexible in the sense that it may allow for add-on capabilities and activities in subsequent updates and be designed, developed, and modified in such a way as to provide a more intense program to address the church's growth needs and overall approach to comprehensive emergency management preparedness and response operations. The appendices to the plan would be designed to give definition to the terms and acronyms used throughout the basic plan and would be the location for any supporting figures, maps, and forms. The emergency support function annexes would focus on the detail of the specific ministry responsibilities and supporting resources.

C. Scope

The scope of the emergency plan defines the emergencies or disasters to which the plan may apply—the various ministries and the geographical location of the church. A hazard/risk matrix will be included in the plan that may be examined and completed for specific hazards as conditions or the environment change. The planning elements should apply to the entire church and membership. It will be emphasized as alluded to above that the church may be affected by an emergency or incident not on the church property but at a remote site or affected by an incident in the nearby neighborhood or region. In a similar instance, the community at large may be adversely affected by a major incident at the church, thus requiring the assistance of local, state, and/or federal assistance.

D. Situation

As the planning dialogue continues, it will be explained that the crisis or emergency situation will describe the "environment" and should clearly identify why the emergency plan is needed. This section of the plan should identify, summarize, and prioritize all hazards faced by the church. The situation should include a brief discussion of the uniqueness of location and a description of the environment or geographical setting. The plan should also provide in general the estimated membership or capacity of the church, allowing for adjustments or increases based on special programs or venues.

E. Assumptions

Assumptions are statements that are assumed as facts for planning purposes in order to execute the emergency plan. Assumptions indicate areas where adjustments to the plan may need to be made as the facts are learned. For instance:

- The church will identify and name the Emergency Planning Coordinator, who will serve as the key individual to coordinate and mobilize resources and personnel as required by the situation.

Theoretical Foundations for the Model

- Incidents are managed at the church level, and in its first or initial assessment would not necessarily involve other churches, the community, or local government.
- The church will consider and may have mutual aid agreements with neighboring churches as deemed or determined appropriate.
- Any special facilities on the church grounds (child-care facilities, scout houses or facilities, vehicle garages, etc.) will come under the jurisdiction of the basic emergency plan.
- Extra resources and assistance will be available from within the local community (e.g., fire and police departments, medical and nursing facilities, emergency rescue squads, and other life agencies).
- The pastor or church administrator within the decision-making chain will be in charge and have the authority to implement the necessary requirements needed within the emergency plan.
- Full cooperation between church officials, auxiliaries, and ministries: administrative staff will be present and trained to support plan implementation.

F. Concept of Operations

The concept of operations should capture the overall approach to the planned response to include:

- The sequence of action;
- Declaration or official statement of emergency;
- Evaluation of requests for resources and determining how these requests will be met, including the use of outside aid;
- Direction and control, including considerations for the incident or primary site incident control and coordination (e.g., office of the pastor or church office);

Crisis and Emergency Management and Preparedness

- Alert and warning considerations and protocol; and
- Response, return, and recovery activities.

G. General

A primary goal of the church is to provide a safe and sacred space for worship and the fulfillment of a broad array of enjoyments proffered by the Divine between God and neighbor. Ultimately, a church is an organization where its members gather around an agreed-upon theme or purpose, and then implement or put in place whatever its members decide to do relative to a given cause or purpose. In this instance, the church consists of an environment of ministerial and lay members, operating in an open forum subject to both internal and external factors and forces.

This section of the crisis and emergency management plan (CEMP) should give an overall summary of the church's plan for response to any emergency or disaster. Using an all-hazards approach, it should identify and provide general information on primary roles and responsibilities of key ministries and of primary actions to be completed. Typically the pastor or chief administrator of the church is responsible for the implementation of the emergency plan. The emergency plan will only be employed when there is an actual or imminent threat to the congregation or to groups who may be using the facility at a particular time. If and when an emergency or crisis occurs, the church will need to be prepared to handle the initial effect of the event until further assistance can be given or until the situation is mitigated. In the event an incident exceeds the church's emergency response capabilities, outside assistance may be available, either through mutual support agreements with other churches, volunteer emergency organizations, and/or the local government.

Theoretical Foundations for the Model

Preparedness

This component includes actions that are developed and implemented during nonemergency or disaster periods that will prepare the church for potential emergency response if and when necessary. They include:

1. Public information and educational materials that will be provided to the various ministerial leaders and staffs and members of the congregation, for example, through church bulletins and special notices;
2. Development, review, and update of components of the church's emergency plan including operational protocol, procedures, and so forth;
3. Development and conduct of training and drills to enhance and ensure readiness of emergency response;
4. Scenario development, drills and exercise requirements, and routine maintenance and performance of emergency resources and equipment; and
5. Assurance of the viability and accuracy of emergency contact lists and maintenance of resource lists and emergency contracts.

Response

Actions in this category are taken to preserve life, property, the environment, and the social and economic structure of the church. Some issues to be considered at this point in the incident are:

- Protection of responder health and safety;
- Fire;
- Emergency medical services;
- Evacuations;
- Dissemination of general (public) information;

Crisis and Emergency Management and Preparedness

- Actions to minimize additional damage;
- Public health and medical services;
- Distribution of emergency supplies; and
- Protection and restoration of critical infrastructure (gas mains, obstructions in exit or evacuation corridors).

Recovery

This component of emergency management and preparedness addresses actions that may occur after the initial response has been implemented, and should be undertaken as soon as possible after the emergency or hazard is terminated. These measures will assist the church leadership and key resource support staff to return the church to normal, or pre-emergency conditions as soon as possible or as much as feasible. During the recovery period, some of the issues that will need to be handled are:

- Behavioral assessment
- Damage assessment
- Cleanup and restoration of the facilities and grounds

Mitigation

These may be current or planned actions that may be under way or designed to reduce or eliminate future risk to the church or congregation. During the mitigation process, these issues should be addressed:

- Hazard (predictive) modeling to protect critical assets;
- Early documentation of losses avoided as a result of previous preparedness and mitigation measures; and
- Congregational education and outreach necessary to improve preparedness, response, and recovery in the event of a future emergency.

Theoretical Foundations for the Model

H. Declaration of an Emergency

The pastor may declare an emergency to exist whenever the threat or actual occurrence of a disaster is or threatens to be of sufficient severity and magnitude to require the cessation of activities, programs, or services or closure of the church in order to prevent or alleviate damage, loss, hardship, or suffering. The emergency may also be declared by any other authorized or designated official of the church.

I. Plan Development and Maintenance

Drafting an emergency plan is a church-wide effort and relies heavily on the church leadership, including its pastor, chief administrators, and leaders of the various ministries—especially the trustees, diaconate, ushers league, and the Board of Christian Education (BCE) or a coordinating arm of the church. Often this work is led by an emergency management expert or planning professional to provide comprehensive guidance to the organization on hazard or risk analysis, exercise design, evacuation planning, and overall emergency preparedness.

Formation of Planning Team

The formation of the planning team is a key function and crucial element in the development of the overall planning process. Organizationally, individuals were selected for the PPBC Emergency Planning Team who represented a good cross-section of the church and its various ministries. The Planning Team consisted of the following key positions and representatives:

- Pastor
- Chair or cochair, Trustees' Ministry
- Chair or cochairs, Board of Christian Education
- Coordinator, Ushers' Ministry

Crisis and Emergency Management and Preparedness

- Coordinator of Safety and Security Committee
- Director of the Health and Medical Services Ministry
- Representatives from external groups:
    - Coordinator of Community Outreach Ministry
    - At-Large Church Members Representatives (two individuals representing the choir ministry and decorum, respectively)

Preliminary Planning Efforts

From the outset of the emergency planning project the pastor's approval and concurrence were found to be key foundational elements and fundamental to the overall planning process. The pastor's team participation and ongoing input and support were essential. All planning issues and proposals were coordinated with the pastor to ensure appropriate communication among and within church ministries. Moreover, the pastor of Providence Park Baptist Church ensured that the Emergency Planning Coordinator was given time on the agenda of church business meetings, where the emergency planning project could be presented, updates on plan status could be offered, comments would be received, and responses could be made to questions dealing with the purpose for the plan.

As the coordinating model for the planning effort, the Board of Christian Education, in conjunction with the Trustees' Ministry, was selected to assume the lead in constructing the planning model, in overall coordination of the planning effort, and for publishing updates of the church's emergency plan. However, it was noted that a similar ministry or individual may be employed to function in this capacity as time went on. It was proposed that the plan would be updated on a four-year basis or whenever it became expedient that changes be made and noted. Plan updates were to be coordinated with each emergency resource group—trustees, diaconate, ushers—to assure proper coordination, development,

Theoretical Foundations for the Model

distribution, and implementation of the appropriate planning elements and sections. The BCE or other individual(s) would also maintain responsibility for training and exercise design to assure that the church's emergency plan is tested or exercised or a drill is conducted on a scheduled or as-needed basis.

It was continuously emphasized throughout the planning coordination process that the objectives for the project were the key elements of the model:

- ***To Awaken:*** Ensure that Providence Park Baptist Church—leadership, ministries, and congregation—is aware of the types of emergencies that are most likely to occur in or around the church.

- ***To Encourage:*** Meaning that the Providence Park Baptist Church Emergency Planning Team would assist the leadership and each member of the congregation to identity and use their gifts and skills in such a manner that one will have something to contribute to the overall cause in the event of a crisis, disaster, or other emergency.

- ***To Equip:*** Using the Providence Park Baptist Church Emergency Plan, persons who have the requisite professional background and talents were made aware that they could be called upon and tasked to offer consultation and training and to prepare other individuals overall to react to an emergency should one occur. Training would be continued through the years, and education should occur as new members and officers were added.

The planning paradigm introduced and implemented with Providence Park Baptist Church, the target community, is as follows:

Awakening Perspective

During the awakening planning mode, the challenges and strengths of the planning effort were presented and explained. We discussed this component with the pastor and respective church leaders and gained their input and support on how best to meet this objective. It was suggested that the most appropriate or beneficial opportunity would be through open forums and sessions, that is, during church conference or business sessions, church executive board meetings, and other special-call meetings where the project will be given time on the agenda. An orientation and emergency planning kit or package was prepared and made available as a handout for all attendees. Extra copies were on hand for those persons unavailable or unable to attend the various schedule orientation sessions.

A key element of the discussion and presentation focused on the history of hazards that have affected the church and/or nearby community. Discussion ensued highlighting disasters that have hit or affected the region—in this case, the City of Richmond metropolitan area and vicinities beyond where church members lived, that is, counties of Chesterfield, Hanover, Henrico, Goochland, Powhatan, New Kent, and Charles City. See Table 1, Hazard Categories and Components, above.

A key focal point of the awakening perspective was on encouraging and receiving feedback, that is, based on questions and response to how various members or family members have been affected by disaster or an emergency, with follow-up on how they responded and what precautions they took in advance of the event, if any. This activity was very helpful. We pointed out that by having an emergency plan, a person or family is likely to have better outcome or survival history than without a plan. We also queried persons to see how many people have an emergency plan and asked them to give testimonials.

The awakening phase concluded with an in-depth look and discussion regarding various church particulars. During this aspect we assessed the nominal age of the congregants; age, size and condition of the infrastructure of the church facility; geographical location; and resource availability or lack thereof within the congregation.

During the awakening phase we also identified persons who were interested in being a part of the Emergency Planning Team. Several persons came forward after the presentation and volunteered to serve on the team. Thankfully, individuals selected and

Theoretical Foundations for the Model

those who volunteered represented a good cross-section of Providence Park Baptist Church and its various ministries.

Encouraging Perspective

The encouraging mode was coupled with the awakening perspective. In practice, this meant we built on and explained the experiences and successes of other church communities or similar organizations such as local governments; took advantage of lessons learned by persons who have experienced a disaster or emergency; and assisted the church leadership and each member of the congregation, regardless of age or gender, to recognize or identify their gifts and skills that may be useful in times of a crisis or emergency. It has been discovered through disaster history—personal stories from events throughout the Commonwealth of Virginia and communities worldwide—that unsuspecting persons contributed tremendous assets and made a significant difference in the saving of lives and property, turning what would have been a major disaster into a minor emergency.

It is expected that the church and congregation will be encouraged knowing that there are people to help in the emergency planning process, persons who have experience in dealing with disasters. That person or those experienced professionals will be able to sort through the core of the problem, assist where there are difficulties or divergent views, and highlight the most important aspects of work to be addressed on a priority basis. Through diplomatic and tactful leadership efforts we will be able to address emergency planning areas that are the most meaningful and relative to Providence Park Baptist Church.

As noted above under the Awakening Perspective section, the church was encouraged by the emergency preparedness presentation, and there appeared to be an eagerness to develop an emergency plan when the people were made aware of the nominal age of the congregation, age and condition of the facility, geographical location, and resources within the congregation. This finding was pointed out on several occasions, and emergency planning

Crisis and Emergency Management and Preparedness

became a major focal point during the encouraging and equipping perspectives. Consequently, the church membership, and the Emergency Planning Team in particular, was encouraged to focus on the key issues such as health and medical needs, evacuation logistics, and assistance to the aged and elderly should there be an emergency at the facility.

Equipping Perspective

The focus of this perspective centered on the development of the Providence Park Baptist Church Emergency Planning Team. The first and most essential step under the equipping mode was to identify and form the Emergency Planning Team.

The next step in this section was to assign the planning team the mission to survey what plans or planning components may exist already for the church rather than start from scratch or re-invent the wheel, so to speak. A planning professional in the area of emergency management was engaged to outline and draft the emergency plan and offer it to the planning team as a "straw man," that is, a template for markup and work purposes. The actual plan development took a considerable amount of time, because it involved coordination, review, and evaluation to ensure that the document addressed each of the planning elements, parameters, and components outlined above. The final draft of the Providence Park Baptist Emergency Plan was limited to the key essentials for the respective target group, and omitted some of the full complement of the traditional or generally accepted emergency planning sections as noted on the pages cited. The extensiveness of the plan depended on two factors: (1) the personal time the team was able to contribute for the initial version of the plan, and (2) the most important planning aspects identified and included during the first round and documented in the first version.

The emergency plan was formatted to include appendices that focused on specific elements of the plan, such as evacuation, health and medical services, and safety and security. It was discussed and noted that other appendices could be considered in the

Theoretical Foundations for the Model

future and developed as may apply to the target church. Equipping the church included design of a site-specific evacuation floor plan. The diagram will show the location of the CPR/AED unit, fire extinguishers, and, of course, evacuation instructions and logistics to ensure proper routing during an emergency.

The equipping perspective also addressed training issues. The team isolated the areas where training was most needed. In addition, this perspective included developing a design for the execution of drills and exercises to test the plan for its viability.

The equipping phase included communications and notices about the church's emergency plan and the role or responsibility of each person to know such things as the evacuation plan, how alerts and warning would be conducted, health and medical services procedures, and the channels and distribution method for official emergency information. This information was provided to church members in printed form via church bulletin inserts. Moreover, announcements and other forms of communication would be updated and continued based on necessity or other factors, such as the prevalence of hazards in the area, community issues or disruptions, weather conditions, and so forth.

The final step under equipping the church was to subject the plan to final review by the church leadership. Upon completion, the plan was distributed and made available to the pastor, key officials of the church, and ministry leaders. One of the final pieces of planning instructions offered under the equipping phase was to encourage the updating of the plan every four years or less as conditions change or emergencies may dictate.

Role of Other Organizations and Support Groups

Role of the Baptist General Convention of Virginia

Early on during project formation we met with Dr. Elisha Burke, director of men's and health ministries, BGCVA, to introduce the project, receive input, and offer emergency planning assistance to the BGCVA. Through coordination with the BGCVA leadership, the project was received enthusiastically and arrangements were subsequently made to provide communication and follow up on opportunities to present workshops on emergency preparedness and planning for the associations and participating churches of the BGCVA. We were very encouraged by Dr. Burke's assistance and the work performed with a number of BGCVA churches. As an outgrowth of those conversations, the project coordinator was contacted to give emergency planning workshop presentations during various sessions of the BGCVA. Also as a result of one of Dr. Burke's suggestions, we reached out to the BGCVA contact in northern Virginia to determine what emergency planning assistance could be rendered in that part of the Commonwealth of Virginia to BGCVA churches.

Role of Contextual Associates

As required by the STVU Doctor of Ministry Program, I contacted several persons to consider becoming a contextual associate in support of this work. The individuals chosen represented a good cross-section of the people who compose the context of my ministry. The contextual associates also represented various educational and professional backgrounds and levels of faith development. I thank each of them for formally making a covenant agreement pledging their guidance, support, time, and resources to this work. Each associate in his or her own way provided feedback on the document, helped me interpret the ministry context, and served as a source of guidance, support, and encouragement during this arduous process.

Measures of Success

Tools used to measure success at end of the project were primarily through means of interviews and group dialogue or discussion. In addition, success was gauged by the extent to which emergency preparedness assistance, presentations, and support were

Theoretical Foundations for the Model

requested by PPBC church ministries or other churches in the Richmond area and beyond.

Timetable of Planning Performance

The Project Scope, Projected Planning Dates, and Level of Activity

The PPBC Emergency Plan Initial Project Brief was scheduled for Wednesday, January 27, 2010, during which an Emergency Planning Committee and Planning Team were discussed and the following ministries and representative areas were identified with the project:

PPBC Emergency Planning Committee members (or representative ministries):

Ministry	Name*	Telephone (or Mobile)	E-mail
Trustees' Ministry	(personal information removed)		
Ushers' Ministry	–	–	–
Scouting Program	–	–	–
Safety and Security	–	–	–
Health and Medical Services	–	–	–
Cooperative Outreach Ministry	–	–	–
Pastor	–	–	–
At-Large Member	–	–	–
At-Large Member	–	–	–
At-Large Member	–	–	–
Project Coordinator	–	–	–

Crisis and Emergency Management and Preparedness

Initial CEMP briefing for PPBC leadership and community:

- January 27, 2010 (Business Meeting)

A minimum of three planning sessions were scheduled:

- March 19, 2010
- June 4, 2010
- July 14, 2010 (Business Meeting)
- September 17, 2010

September 30, 2010, was established as the target due date for the draft completion of the Providence Park Baptist Church Emergency Plan, with the final due one month later.

Activities Chart

This chart represents person-hours by ministry participating in emergency plan-related business meetings, planning meetings, work sessions, small group planning sessions, and training sessions.

Theoretical Foundations for the Model

Ministry	Name	Hours on Assignment (estimated total ministry)
Trustees' Ministry	–	30
Ushers' Ministry	–	60
Scouting Program	–	10
Safety and Security	–	100 hours (including work on a previous Safety and Security Plan)
Health and Medical Services	–	70
Cooperative Outreach Ministry	–	6
Pastor	–	40
At-Large Member	–	6
At-Large Member	–	10
At-Large Member	–	10
Project Coordinator	–	200

4

Engaging the Task and Assigning Responsibilities

Field Experience

Statement of Purpose

IN THIS CHAPTER THE reader is invited to assess the implementation side of the Vonvolkenburg model described in chapter 3 consistent with the planning objectives identified and the preparedness activities undertaken and completed by the target group. Here I describe what actually occurred and was performed during the emergency planning process and the work of the Providence Park Baptist Church Emergency Planning Team.

    Development of a cadre of trained volunteers and subject matter experts from within Providence Park Baptist Church was initially the primary effort toward building a strategically sound and practical emergency plan. It is a fairly well-known phenomenon that these are two areas—volunteerism and identification of in-house or resident-trained professionals in most churches—of greatest challenge when seeking commitment and cooperation. History has shown that individuals and/or communities often do not sense the need to plan for or collaborate and coordinate efforts until or after a catastrophe or disaster has occurred. Even then,

Engaging the Task and Assigning Responsibilities

most communities are clueless on where to turn or how to proceed in organizing to help alleviate or mitigate similar occurrences or situations that may lie ahead.

One of the keys to successful emergency planning within the context of the local church is to identify early on persons who will volunteer their services and commit to the overall preparedness, response, and recovery parameters of a crisis or emergency environment. Because it is quite unlikely—perhaps even unpractical—for the local government to have sufficient personnel to respond to every emergency situation in a timely fashion, church leaders and community volunteers must come forward and avail themselves of training opportunities, emergency coordination and leadership skills development, and other aspects of crisis and emergency preparedness. In most congregations there are persons with requisite skills as a result of prior military service and training, retired first responders, paramedical experience, and so forth. These combined assets can become a critical and vast army of church and community support when properly trained and coordinated. Countless lessons from the past tell us that "when a disaster strikes, public emergency resources cannot satisfy the extensive needs, but they can be supplemented by volunteers, charitable institutions. . . . With proper preparation and coordination, it is possible to integrate the private and public emergency forces."[1]

This early first effort—identifying persons to participate in the emergency planning process—involved discussions with the church leadership including the pastor and leaders of key ministries—trustees, diaconate, and Board of Christian Education. Subsequent to this dialogue and obtaining tentative approval to proceed, a PowerPoint presentation was prepared and, with the concurrence of the pastor, an Emergency Preparedness Orientation Session was scheduled. This presentation was given at the church business meeting on January 27, 2010, which was attended by approximately seventy members of the congregation. Providence Park Baptist Church is blessed with several persons who had the initiative and volunteered to support the emergency team

---

1. Blackstone and Hakim, "It Takes a Village," 40, 42–43.

Crisis and Emergency Management and Preparedness

effort. A civil service professional who teaches criminal justice and sociology at Virginia State University eagerly joined the team. That member encouraged and led others to join or be a part of the team effort. The church also has a medical doctor as one of its members, who took the lead on developing and updating the health and medical services procedures. Several team members have experience in criminal justice, safety and security, human resources, and personnel management. It is anticipated that the team will continue to flourish in months and years to come, and especially as others come to the awareness that disasters and hazards are not going away.

Project Target

As outlined in chapter 3, the planning paradigm was threefold:

- *To Awaken:* Ensure that Providence Park Baptist Church—leadership, ministries, and congregation—is aware of the types of emergencies that are most likely to occur in or around the church.

- *To Encourage:* Meaning that the Providence Park Baptist Church Emergency Planning Team would assist the leadership and each member of the congregation to identity and use their gifts and skills in such a manner that one will have something to contribute to the overall cause in the event of a crisis, disaster, or other emergency.

- *To Equip:* Using the Providence Park Baptist Church Emergency Plan, persons who have the requisite professional background and talents were made aware that they could be called upon and tasked to offer consultation and training and to prepare other individuals overall to react to an emergency should one occur. Training would be continued through the years, and education should occur as new members and officers were added.

Engaging the Task and Assigning Responsibilities

It was discovered and reported that the church (Christian community) can effect positive interactions among and within the human enterprise, that is, its mission is to participate with the Divine Eternal in creating a new heaven and new earth. It is at the center of the effort to reconcile that lost primal relationship with God. The church—God/humanity dynamic—is the covenant-based centerpiece of our existence, founded on Jesus Christ, Son of the Living God, and the sole purpose of the function of the church in the world.

The Providence Park Baptist Church Emergency Planning Team initially identified and engaged a modified partnered or collaborative-coordinated approach to emergency preparedness. The original planning intent on the part of myself, the project coordinator, was to involve the five churches of the Cooperative Outreach Ministry (COM) in the planning effort. As noted elsewhere in this project document, the five churches are: First Baptist Church, Washington Park; Good Hopewell Baptist Church, Florida Avenue; Providence Park Baptist Church, Providence Park; Seventh Street Baptist Church, Meadowbridge Road; and St. John Baptist Church, Washington Park. However, it was determined that during the initial emergency planning effort the energy would be focused primarily on developing an emergency plan for Providence Park Baptist Church. This modification to the planning intent did not weaken the effort; if anything, by concentrating on the overall goal and objectives and narrowing the focus to include only Providence Park Baptist Church, the overall effort was enhanced and strengthened for the target community. It was discussed that expanding the Emergency Planning Team effort to include other churches could be a later option. The local representative for the five-church Cooperative Outreach Ministry would continue as a member of the planning team.

Crisis and Emergency Management and Preparedness

Project Documentation (Write-Up)

Project Findings and Observations

A. Overall Mission

To enhance life safety at the Providence Park Baptist Church

B. Project Goal

To develop an Emergency Management and Preparedness Plan for Providence Park Baptist Church, the target community

C. Specific Objectives

To Awaken:

Ensure that the Providence Park Baptist Church—leadership, ministries and congregation—is aware of the types of emergencies that are most likely to occur in or around the church.

This objective was achieved through planning sessions, printed handout and materials distributed to the membership at large, presentations at the Church Business Session, and other details as follow.

Project Proposal

During the awareness mode the challenges and strengths of the planning effort were presented and explained. There was broad interest by persons who attended the church business meetings, and many offered comments to the project coordinator both during the business sessions and after the meetings. Planning components were discussed with the

Engaging the Task and Assigning Responsibilities

pastor and respective church leaders to gain their input on how best to meet the overall planning objectives.

Project Presentation

A strategy was outlined to engage the various church ministries and, by using the trustee and diaconate liaisons communication and coordination of the planning effort, was widespread and known to all. Open forums and sessions, that is, during church conference or business sessions, church executive board meetings, and other special call meetings, were very beneficial to the project. Of course, the pastor demonstrated outstanding leadership by providing a window of opportunity on business and meeting agendas for planning updates and status reports.

Congregational Information

An orientation and emergency planning kit was packaged and made available as handouts at meetings for attendees. Extra packages were made unavailable for persons unable to attend the awareness sessions. The PowerPoint presentation was given. A key element of the discussion and presentation focused on the history of hazards that have affected Providence Park Baptist Church and the nearby community. Particular effort was made to highlight disasters that have hit or affected the region, in this case, the City of Richmond metropolitan area, and vicinities beyond where church members reside, that is, counties of Chesterfield, Hanover, Henrico, Goochland, Powhatan, New Kent, and Charles City.

Hazard Identification

A key focal point of the awareness mode was to promote and receive feedback, that is, based on questions and response

Crisis and Emergency Management and Preparedness

to how various members or family members have been affected by disaster or an emergency, with follow-up on how they responded and what precautions they took in advance of the event, if any. This was a good exchange, and demonstrated particular interest in local emergencies. It was pointed out that by having an emergency plan, a person or family is likely to have better outcome from the effects of a disaster than without a plan. Several persons were very forthcoming with testimonials of how they have survived prior disasters and emergencies.

Planning Solutions

The awareness objective concluded with an in-depth look and discussion regarding various church particulars. The nominal age of the congregants was observed to be an important aspect of the emergency plan. Also the condition of the infrastructure of the church—electrical and heating systems, gas mains, and so forth—were assessed to ensure these systems were addressed in the plan.

The planning team discussed and agreed to narrow the focus of the emergency plan to two very specific areas:

- *Evacuation Planning*
- *Health and Medical Services Element*

To Encourage:

Meaning that the Providence Park Baptist Church Emergency Planning Team would assist the leadership and each member of the congregation to identity and use their gifts and skills in such a manner that one will have something to contribute to the overall cause in the event of a crisis, disaster, or other emergency. The church and team were encouraged through efforts made to promote and use:

Engaging the Task and Assigning Responsibilities

Resource Availability

This objective was achieved by inviting and having church leaders and pastor participate in planning meeting and team work session. Several one-on-one small group teams met to plan details on the key focus areas.

Providence Park Baptist Church is blessed with having a practicing medical doctor as a member of the church family, who took the lead working out the details for health and medical services ministry and orchestrating medical services training.

Several subgroup sessions were held with the chairperson of the Trustees' Ministry to scope out the evacuation scheme and logistics. Two evacuation orientation sessions were held with more than 75 percent participation by key ministries.

The encouraging mode was coupled with the awareness perspective. In practice, this meant that we built on and took advantage of experiences and successes of other church communities or similar organizations such as local governments, gained from lessons learned by persons who have experienced a disaster or emergency, and assisted the church leadership and each member of the congregation to recognize or identify their gifts and skills that may be useful in times of a crisis or emergency.

Resource Identification

It was pointed out on several occasions that the church and congregation were encouraged knowing the church body had members who were professionals in the medical field, emergency management and preparedness, and crisis counseling—persons who had experience in dealing with disasters. Those persons were able to sort through the core of the problem, assist where there were difficulties or divergent views about how to tackle a particular problem, and highlight the most important aspects of work to be addressed on a priority basis. Through diplomatic and tactful leadership efforts we were able to address emergency planning areas that turned out to be the most meaningful and relative to Providence Park Baptist Church.

Resource Appreciation

As noted above, under the awareness objective church members voiced words of encouragement and were seemingly excited to attend and participate in a church that took emergency preparedness seriously. It was also noted by team members and others that they were very encouraged that the church and the emergency plan prioritized its focus to address key congregational issues such as health and medical needs, evacuation logistics, and assistance to the elderly should there be an emergency at the facility.

To Equip:

Using the Providence Park Baptist Church Emergency Plan, persons who have the requisite professional background and talents were made aware that they could be called upon and tasked to offer consultation and training and to prepare other individuals overall to react to an emergency should one occur. Training would be continued through the years, and education should occur as new members and officers were added.

This objective was achieved primarily by the formation of the planning team; development, publication, and distribution of the Providence Park Baptist Church Emergency Plan and training documents. Specifically, the equipping phase was satisfied as follows:

Engaging the Task and Assigning Responsibilities

Planning Team Formation

The focus of the equipping objective centered on the development of the Providence Park Baptist Church Emergency Planning Team as the first and most essential step. The team consisted of the pastor and the following ministries or church representatives:

- Trustees' Ministry representative
- Ushers' Ministry representative
- Scouting Program representative
- Safety and security representative
- Health and Medical Services representative
- Cooperative Outreach Ministry representative
- At-large (two members)

The planning team logged in more than 542 hours on the project. (see the Timetable of Planning Performance near the end of chapter 3).

Planning Team Assignments

The next step in terms of equipping was to assign the planning team the mission to survey what plans or planning components existed prior to the subject project and build on these prior efforts rather than start from scratch or reinvent the wheel. A planning professional in the area of emergency management was engaged to outline and draft a "straw man" emergency plan and offer it to the planning team as a template for markup and work purposes. The actual plan development process occurred over a period of ten months, from January through October 2010.

Crisis and Emergency Management and Preparedness

Plan Development

The final design and format of the Providence Park Baptist Church Emergency Plan was narrowed from the full complement of planning components to address three key elements—evacuation, health and medical services, and building safety and security—with particular focus on the first two elements. It was agreed that the plan could be modified or expanded in future years to address other important aspects as may be determined by congregational requirements, disaster history, and so forth.

Version 1 (October 30, 2010) of the PPBC Emergency Plan was formatted to include appendices to focus on specific elements of the plan such as evacuation, health and medical services, and safety and security. This modified format was agreed to by the church leadership. Equipping the church meant development of a site-specific evacuation floor plan, including the location of the CPR/AED unit, fire extinguishers, and, of course, evacuation instructions and logistics in the layout to ensure effective communications and proper routing during an emergency.

Plan Exercise and Training

The equipping perspective also addressed training issues. The team isolated areas where training was most needed such as health and medical training in the administration and use of CPR/AED apparatus. The equipping mode included a design for the execution of drills and exercises to test the plan for its viability. Two drills and orientation sessions were conducted to test the feasibility of the plan and practicality in implementation.Communications and notices regarding the availability and use of the emergency plan were announced to the church membership via the various ministries. Notices to membership are placed in church bulletins on how they would be notified in the event

Engaging the Task and Assigning Responsibilities

of an emergency and how persons may contact the church or other authorities in a time of emergency. The church has (1) a communications plan and system of how alerts and warnings will be given, and (2) health and medical services procedures on how this ministry will provide aid and comfort to those in need. The church has a health and medical care center off the main sanctuary.

Plan Acceptance and Distribution

The final step under equipping the church was submission of the plan to the church leadership for final approval. Although unsigned at the time of this document publication, the plan is essentially approved for use in a crisis or emergency. The final plan was produced in a bound 8.5-inch x 11-inch format along with several 5-inch x 7-inch bound booklets that proved handy for carrying, and so forth. Also, the document was made available to the church clerk in electronic format for further publication and distribution as the need may arise.

Plan Maintenance

One of the final pieces of planning instructions offered under the equipping phase was to explain the necessity of ensuring that the plan is maintained and updated every four years or less as conditions changes or emergencies may dictate. This instruction was well received.

Planning Summary

The contextual problem identified early on was the lack or need to build community or shared fellowship to address disasters or emergencies that may or could affect the church, and especially the African American church community, specifically Providence Park Baptist Church. As noted above under the model planning objectives, the scope of the planning effort was narrowed to include primary emphasis on three areas: (1) health and medical care and support services, (2) evacuation and training, and (3) emergency plan development for the church. The goal of the project was achieved and the objectives were satisfied.

Leadership strengths related to the contextual problem were found resident in a unique awareness for and the ability to identify and enhance principles of accountability among and between the corporate church and individual members within the fellowship. The planning approach was fivefold:

1. Build cooperation to accomplish this object or broad purpose of the project;
2. Explain necessity for and model personal accountability toward that end;
3. Expect and appreciate unpretentious characteristics in others through cooperative interfaces and interactions;
4. Communicate and collaborate with others through multidimensional and multidisciplinary means of loyalty, trust, and responsibility; and
5. Employ project management skills responsibly that focus attention on ethics within team building and membership.

The objectives or project team elements enumerated above were accomplished through faithful participation in the planning process and further enhanced though the use of unique aspects of varying leadership skill sets among the planning team. To the project's advantage, it was discovered that the project included a broad and rich cross-section of leadership styles, for example:

a. Analytical and definitional leadership;
b. Conflict adjusting or compensational leadership;
c. Democratic-centered with a view toward empowerment;
d. Reconciliational leadership;
e. Situational, that is, based on mission, task, and resources; and

f. Transformational leadership, that is, that focuses on liberty for the oppressed and suffering, redistribution or sharing of resources, and so forth.

Key leadership attributes or qualities characterized or demonstrated in the models or styles noted above included elements of preaching/teaching, that is, *kerygma* (telling); caregiving, that is, *diakonia* (doing); and community/life working (praxis) together, that is, *koinonia* (lifestyle). Moreover within the ministerial context, emphasis was placed on shared leadership, empowerment of lay ministries, advocacy, institutional governance (through polity boards, committees, etc.), corporate and individual responsibility, human/social services entities within neighborhood, and prophetic action vis-à-vis life-demanding/threatening potentialities.

One can often find reasons to celebrate. For example, when the CPR/AED training was held on one early Saturday morning, reluctant volunteers warmed up to the idea of training when it was discovered that they were being treated to a healthy breakfast and delightful lunch. Perhaps herein is a lesson: providing breakfast, lunch, or refreshments may be just the thing to encourage some individuals to attend training sessions. Emergency planning can be fun, and in the end can provide the opportunity to celebrate accomplishments engendered through fellowship and the sharing of gifts and skills with the knowledge that planning, training, and working together may help save lives.

Emergency Management and Preparedness Planning Team: Activities and Meetings

The Providence Park Baptist Church Emergency Preparedness (EP) Planning Committee was approved at an official meeting of the church on January 27, 2010. It was recognized that a church safety committee was started a few years before, and that the new team would work to incorporate and restructure the efforts undertaken by that group. Indeed, some of the members of the previous safety committee were named to the Emergency Planning

Committee. The new EP Planning Team used prior information and built on it so as not to "reinvent the wheel," so to speak. An EP scoping session was held on March 27, 2010, and became the first EP Planning Team meeting.

As noted above under the equipping phase, the PPBC EP Planning Team was composed of the following ministries and representatives:

- Trustees' Ministry representative
- Ushers' Ministry representative
- Scouting Program representative
- Safety and security representative
- Health and Medical Services representative
- Cooperative Outreach Ministry representative
- At-large (two members)

The second in a series of Emergency Planning Committee meetings was held June 4, 2010, at Providence Park Baptist Church. As a follow-up to the March 27, 2010, scoping session, the committee consisting of eleven members of various ministries and from the church at large reviewed the PPBC EP Draft (June 4, 2010) Plan, discussed key elements, and agreed on a planning basis and format to address the greatest near-term needs for this particular African American church and community. The draft plan was prepared by the project coordinator.

Engaging the Task and Assigning Responsibilities

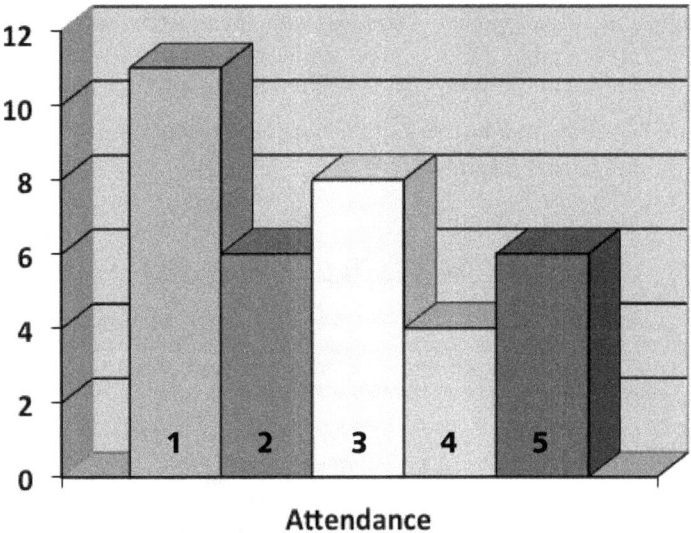

Attendance

Figure 1. Attendance averaged 43 percent overall. This equates favorably with the overall national EP preparedness interest level. See Figure 2 below.

1 January 27, 2010: Emergency Planning (EP) Organizational Meeting

2 March 27, 2010: EP Team Meeting (54 percent attendance based on commitment at organizational meeting)

3 June 4, 2010: EP Team Meeting (72 percent attendance based on commitment at organizational meeting)

4 September 10, 2010: EP Team Meeting (36 percent attendance based on commitment at organizational meeting)

5 October 30, 2010: EP Meeting and Training Exercise (54 percent attendance based on commitment at organizational meeting)

Crisis and Emergency Management and Preparedness

By unanimous consent, the team of leaders and lay members agreed that the following two areas were the most urgent:

- Health and Medical Services Procedures and Training; and
- Evacuation Plan, including Support Personnel and Warning Protocols.

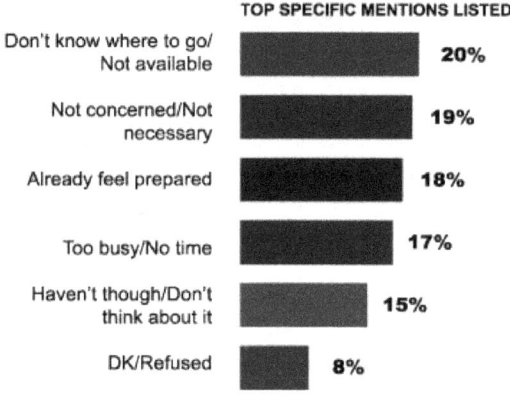

Figure 2. Barriers to being prepared.[2]

2. While some may consider this statistic a dreadful potent of the state of preparedness, this author along with others in the business of emergency management assess these percentages as positive trends compared with the would-be state of preparedness in the absence or lack of planning by any organization. In the December 2004 issue of *The Wirthlin Report*, researchers noted that "Americans need to take the initiative and become more prepared for a disaster instead of waiting to react to a disaster after the fact. Despite the gaps between what people know and what they do, there is hope" ("U.S. Public Unprepared," 4).

Engaging the Task and Assigning Responsibilities

Cardio Pulmonary Resuscitation and Automatic External Defibrillator (CPR/AED) training was offered and conducted Saturday, June 26, 2010, at the church. Including the instructor and facilitator, twelve persons participated in this emergency preparedness training session.

The planning committee discussed the need to provide for essential equipment, materials, and supplies. Included in the discussion was the requirement for an emergency generator, adequate fire extinguishers, and so forth. It was agreed that the church had some supplies and other essentials could be added at a later time.

At the September 10, 2010, EP planning meeting, the team established a process whereby subgroups would work to develop and refine the two crucial planning components (Health-Medical and Evacuation) on parallel tracks. The emphasis was placed on the Health and Medical Services element as the most critical considering the median age of the church membership. It was also agreed that since the EP plan would, by necessity, contain sensitive information specific to PPBC and its community, selected personal and proprietary information would be blocked out and not published in this project. Of course, key excerpts and an outline of the Providence Park Baptist Church Emergency Plan would be shown as an example of the extent of work involved in the development of a comprehensive crisis and emergency management and preparedness plan for a church.

One of the keys to success is communication. At the July 14, 2010, PPBC Biannual Church Meeting, George Urquhart, the project manager and coordinator of the PPBC Emergency Planning Committee, reported that the committee met on June 4, 2010 to follow up on objectives as outlined at the January 27, 2010, biannual church meeting. The notes of that meeting were recorded and are held by the church clerk. It was noted that the director of Health and Medical Services (a member of the church and local doctor) would develop a plan and comprehensive procedures to be used in medical emergencies at the church. The Health and Medical Services Plan would require that there should be a team of four health ministry people on duty every Sunday—at least one will be

Crisis and Emergency Management and Preparedness

trained and proficient in CPR and AED operation and administration. This detail is captured and documented in the PPBC EP Plan. The evacuation planning effort focused on the safety and security aspects of the process as well as protocol of alerting and warning. It was suggested and agreed that there still needs to be more volunteers to be stationed around the church to help with evacuation plan implementation. Certain issues associated with evacuation of the church facility were voiced such as how extensive it would be, that is, would this action call for the entirety of the church building, meeting rooms, offices to be vacated? What kind of hazards or risks would cause evacuation? It was suggested that the location of the fire extinguishers and the Automated External Defibrillator (AED) unit would be shown on the evacuation plan diagram and layout. It was also agreed that an injury and accident report was an essential and that it would be developed, reviewed, and included in the EP plan. These factors and issues helped establish reasons to prepare and give priority to the completion of the emergency plan. Each of these steps and suggestions have been completed and performed as of this writing.

On October 30, 2010, the EP Planning Team met and held an evacuation training exercise overview. The discussion consisted of a review of the critical areas for evacuation of church. The purpose was twofold: (1) provide an overview of the evacuation process, and (2) and serve as a precursor or prelude to further training on evacuation procedures for the church leadership and membership. Subsequently, a training session on evacuation procedures was held on January 22, 2011, with the Ushers' Ministry and other church leaders. Outstanding participation was observed and was reportedly of great benefit to all in attendance.

Special thanks are extended to the PPBC leadership and Emergency Preparedness Planning Team. The EP Planning Team finalized the draft PPBC Emergency Plan, dated September 30, 2010. The document was subject to review and the final plan is dated October 30, 2010.

Success Achieved

The outcome of the project and planning objectives were successfully achieved based on six measures:

- *Attendance at planning sessions*: Attendance averaged 43 percent overall. This equates favorably with the overall national EP preparedness interest level (see Figures 1 and 2 above).

- *Development/Finalization of the PPBC Emergency Plan*: A target date was set for September 30, 2010, for completion of the draft PPBC Emergency Plan. That time frame was satisfied. More important, the final PPBC Emergency Plan was published October 30, 2010, and made available to the church leadership and members of the PPBC Emergency Planning Team.

- *Conduct of Drills, Exercises and Training*:
    - CPR/AED training was offered and conducted Saturday, June 26, 2010, at the church. Including the instructor and facilitator, twelve persons participated in this emergency preparedness training session. Additional training sessions are planned.

    - Evacuation orientation consisting of drills and exercises were conducted on two occasions: October 30, 2010, and January 22, 2011. Key ministry leaders attended both sessions with substantial participation by essential personnel. Follow-up dialogue with attendees resulted in agreement that this activity was extremely important, timely, and valuable.

- *Interviews*: Met with members of key ministries—trustees, ushers, diaconate, Board of Christian Education, and others—who all, without exception, expressed their appreciation for the overall emergency planning effort and how Providence Park Baptist Church will benefit from this life safety accomplishment.

Crisis and Emergency Management and Preparedness

- *Group Discussion*: The Board of Christian Education, a body of ministry leaders, entertained and welcomed comments on the success of the PPBC emergency planning effort. All comments were very positive. The body expressed thanks to the EP project coordinator and team.

- *Requests for Emergency Planning Assistance (Based on Acknowledged Success of the PPBC EP Effort*: Upon hearing and observing the success of the PPBC emergency planning effort, the project coordinator received an invitation and gave (April 19, 2011) a presentation on the work of PPBC to a neighboring church community. A modified PowerPoint presentation titled "Faithful Readiness," combined with questions and comments, was very well received. Some twenty-five persons attended this neighborhood gathering of church members, neighbors, and friends.

5
Summary, Reflections, and Conclusions

DISASTERS AND EMERGENCIES ARE occurring at an alarming rate, and no community, organization or individual is immune from the devastating effects. In this concluding chapter, I present the summary, reflections, and conclusions of the project. As demonstrated and presented in this document, this project has attempted to confront the realities of disasters and emergencies by helping to prepare a local church for such an occurrence by making the community aware of the likelihood of a crisis, by encouraging the community to recognize its own strengths, and through equipping the entity with intellectual skills and capitalizing on untapped local resources. The concern is that the uniquely cohesive nature of the African American community may disappear into a state of nonexistence as a result of lack of planning and preparedness in the face of natural disasters (floods, hurricanes, tornadoes, severe weather, and so forth) and other disasters and threats ranging from acute economic crises to social inequities. Communities, especially predominant African American communities, are vulnerable to any number of risks and threats, from natural disasters to human-caused incidents, pandemic disease outbreaks, and so forth. Moreover, these communities have more than their share of crime, violence, and social disorders. The African American community has traditionally depended on the local church for assistance in times of need.

The greatest disasters in the world are not always the huge catastrophes that grab the headlines. There are more disasters that involve one person or one family than the headline grabbers. The church cannot minister during the large disasters and ignore the needs of those suffering through individual crises. The greatest tool the kingdom of God has in the world is Christians living in the local community sharing their faith day in and day out with friends and neighbors. The local church ministering in the community is still God's beginning point for the preaching of the gospel of God.

Local churches are in a unique position to respond to individual needs in ways that no other organization or group can. Churches can demonstrate the love of God as they meet the needs of victims in the time of disaster. Even spontaneous reaction to a disaster in or near the church community can be helpful if it is coordinated with disaster relief agencies' response efforts. However, without a coordinated emergency preparedness plan, churches are ill-equipped to respond to any disaster or emergency in their community, whether large or small, in terms of level of disruption or population affected. An effective emergency plan must be well defined, discussed, and exercised by the church leaders. Training must be offered, and team leaders must familiarize themselves with implementation protocol and unique congregational requirements. In addition, the congregation needs to be involved and represented in the planning process as well as be informed and participate in drills and exercises at least annually or semiannually.

Lessons Learned

A. The baseline effort or initiative for disaster and emergency preparedness is founded on three fundamental principles:

1. Actuality or reality that dictates an emergency is likely to affect the individual, facility, or enterprise;

Summary, Reflections, and Conclusions

    2. Awareness that it is not a matter of where but when; and

    3. Assurance that emergency preparedness will help protect lives and property.

B. A local church, including the leadership and key ministries, will be more inclined to work toward the development of the emergency plan when there is appropriate guidance than otherwise. Although Providence Park Baptist Church had a scheme in place for years for evacuation, procedures for health and medical services, and an outline for a Safety and Security Plan, these three disparate planning components were brought together under one umbrella emergency plan as noted in this document, thus ensuring a more coordinated approach to emergency response following authorized protocol standards than likely would be the case in the absence of a comprehensive planning document.

C. If you understand the effect of disasters on the church/human community, and can speak the language of crisis and emergency management and preparedness, you and your audience will understand more quickly risk factors, perceive vulnerabilities, and work more collaboratively to develop a practical emergency preparedness plan than would be the case where this awareness and knowledge did not exist.

D. Church leaders play a key and valuable role in emergency preparedness through strong support and involvement in the process. Ongoing support of the project by the church leadership was found to be essential to a successful planning effort in the local church.

E. Emergency planning and the components of overall emergency preparedness—plan development, training, drills, and exercises—will prove successful when there is wholehearted investment by the church leadership. The pastor of Providence Park Baptist Church and the leaders of the key ministries—Board of Christian Education, trustees, diaconate—faithfully gave of their time and energy to the project by attending meetings, providing input on the development of the emergency plan, and participating in training sessions.

F. Finding or tapping volunteers with the requisite skill sets will continue to be a challenge. In this light, the planning team recognized that there is a continuing need for persons to give of their time and talents to church work, including steadfastness to the commitment of emergency preparedness and ongoing training demands.

G. Leadership challenges included finding moments of cohesiveness (interest) and maintenance of momentum. That meant finding balance between the inner and other self but also between confession of faith and practice. There were times of differences during committee meetings. However, the planning team and the church leadership regarded personal discipline as an essential requirement for accomplishment of task. One of the key findings observed of the project effort was that when the team leader and other project stakeholders demonstrate or model aspiring and ethical leadership qualities, one can usually expect others will sense the urgency or necessity of the cause (project) and find individual basis for ownership as well.

Project Modeling

The planning paradigm focused specifically on the application and employment of the three-step Vonvolkenberg model that resulted in the preparation and execution of an Emergency Preparedness Plan for Providence Park Baptist Church. The planning components and elements were custom designed and tailored to satisfy the church's unique situation. The plan was coordinated and designed overall to address the relevant planning components and elements consistent with generally accepted and nationally

Summary, Reflections, and Conclusions

recognized emergency planning guidance. The mission of the project was satisfied:

> To assist Providence Park Baptist Church to prepare for a disaster or emergency by developing a strategy, incorporated in an emergency plan, to minister to its congregation during crisis through preparing the church, training key leaders and ministries, securing supplies, and developing protocols that will activate the emergency plan in time of need.

An additional outgrowth of the project included the design, development, and presentation of an emergency preparedness orientation program for the Baptist General Convention of Virginia (BGCVA) and a model crisis and emergency management and preparedness (CEMP) planning outline using Providence Park Baptist Church—the target community—as an example.

Past experience has demonstrated that emergencies can quickly turn into crises if it appears that the affected entity—be it federal, state, or local government, or a local church—is not on top of the situation. Although crises and emergencies require different approaches, both types of situations involve many stakeholders and thus represent a tremendous challenge to coordinate unique and often peculiar organizational and communication demands. It is noted far and wide that "when disasters occur, it is people who make the difference. Organizations are just tools. They help us to coordinate and work together, but their effectiveness (or lack thereof) is in the individuals who sit behind the desks, answer the telephones and drive the trucks."[1]

Crisis and emergency management involves timely and effective collaboration between the leader(s), agencies, or ministries. In such a context, the key to a successful response is the ability of the leadership to coordinate efforts with respect to communication and coordination. The purpose of this project was to build confidence and engage the target church to view the threat as an opportunity and, in so doing, to make it aware of the emergency

---

1. Brown, *Our Father's World*, 169.

culture, build confidence and encourage the leaders and congregation, and develop and equip the church through the concept of emergency management and preparedness. A voice of experience notes, "We should work together in and through our church families to involve others and to multiply our efforts."[2]

Project Challenges

Two areas of greatest challenge in this project for me are worth noting. The first challenge I personally encountered was the matter of how to garner the support of the five community churches and rally their interest in emergency preparedness. I considered this the ideal community and target for emergency preparedness in keeping with the idea that more can be accomplished together than a single church acting alone, and particularly since these five churches were already partners in the Community Outreach Ministry. However, almost from the outset through discussions with the target church leadership and coaching by my academic advisor, a decision was reached to focus our preparedness efforts initially on Providence Park Baptist Church, with an eye toward application of the planning model to the other four community churches in the future.

Another challenge I faced was that I had to carve out time that did not conflict with my official employment to meet occasionally with key members of the target church Emergency Planning Team. This subgroup committee work between me, as the project coordinator, and key team members was absolutely essential in order to maximize the time the full committee could meet and work on the overall planning elements.

Finally, and perhaps a challenge of sorts, the reader should understand, as has been stated throughout this document, that the best planning effort would be one where a group of local churches plan together for purposes of marshaling community resources and support in time of crisis or emergency. The size of the group

2. Ibid.

Summary, Reflections, and Conclusions

or consortium of churches would, of course, vary based on demographics and geography or other factors locally considered and selected. However, as stated in this document, the PPBC Emergency Planning Team decided to limit or narrow the initial emergency planning focus and energies to the development of the Providence Park Baptist Church Emergency Plan and not include on this first round other local area church partners. The option would remain open for PPBC and its Emergency Planning Team to share their EP experience with neighbors.

Appendix:

Model Emergency Management and Preparedness Planning:

Providence Park Baptist Church, an African American Church Community within the Commonwealth of Virginia

CRISIS and EMERGENCY MANAGEMENT PLANNING

in association with

Providence Park Baptist Church
468 East Ladies Mile Road
Richmond, Virginia 23222

and

Baptist General Convention of Virginia (BGCVA)

EMERGENCY MANAGEMENT PLANNING

Goal:

Assist and encourage churches in **PREPARATION** for disaster by developing an emergency preparedness culture and strategy to minister to the community during times of crisis through preparing facilities, training, securing supplies, and developing protocols to activate respective disaster response plans.

Objective:

To develop an EMERGENCY MANAGEMENT & PREPAREDNESS PLAN **BEFORE** a disaster occurs in coordination with other churches, local government, and volunteer organizations.

What Is a CRISIS?

A "CRISIS" is a situation that somehow challenges the public's sense of appropriateness, tradition, values, safety, security, or the integrity of the entity or organization, whether by fear of unknown consequences, terror, etc.

What Is a DISASTER?

A "disaster" is anything that causes human suffering or creates human needs that the victims cannot alleviate themselves.

EMERGENCY MANAGEMENT PLANNING

What Is an EMERGENCY?

An "emergency" is something UNFORESEEN and REQUIRES IMMEDIATE ATTENTION and ACTION. It may be any occurrence or imposing threat—natural (act of God) or man-made—that results or may result in substantial harm to people and/or property.

What Is PREPAREDNESS?

"Preparedness" is a FUNCTION that embraces and requires LEADERSHIP, TRAINING, READINESS, and SUPPORT to recognize, prevent, and react to an emergency.

CRISIS and EMERGENCY MANAGEMENT PLAN
(Model Outline)

for

Providence Park Baptist Church

in association with

Baptist General Convention of Virginia

Affiliated Associations

Participating Local Churches

This document is intended for use as a template for local church leaders in developing a site-specific plan for the church. Every church will have different needs, thus the recommendations herein may be adapted to fit the needs of different church communities. For instance, smaller churches may not be able to form a full emergency response team; however, church leaders may be designated to serve in particular functions. Once procedures have been established, it is important that they be relayed to church members and emphasized as often as possible (e.g., church-wide meetings, trainings, drills).

Providence Park Baptist Church
Crisis and Emergency Management Preparedness (CEMP) Plan

CEMP Team
Key Stakeholder Ministries Participation

Primary Ministries

Development and Review
Key Agencies

Internal Reviews

Approval, Publication, and Dissemination/Distribution

Plan Components

Executive Statement (Resolution)*

Basic Plan
- Appendixes
- Emergency Support Annexes
- Support Annexes
- Special Facilities and Functions

*Plan should be updated on a four-year basis and certified current by approving authority or governing body.

Providence Park Baptist Church
Crisis and Emergency Management Preparedness (CEMP) Plan

Uses an "All-Hazards" Approach to Incident Management

Describes the Concepts and Structures of Response and Recovery Operations

Identifies ministries and offices with essential (PRIMARY) and supporting (SUPPORT) emergency management functions

Assigns Emergency Prevention, Preparedness, and Response and Recovery Duties and Responsibilities to Various Ministries and Offices

Four Steps in the Planning Process*

1. Establish a Planning Team
2. Analyze Capabilities and Hazards
3. Develop the Plan
4. Implement the Plan

All planning activities should be tracked and posted in a planning log.

Crisis and Emergency Management Preparedness

Categories of Hazards and Risks*

- Historical
- Geographical
- Technological
- Human Error
- Physical

For purposes of risk analysis and modeling

Providence Park Baptist Church
Crisis and Emergency Management

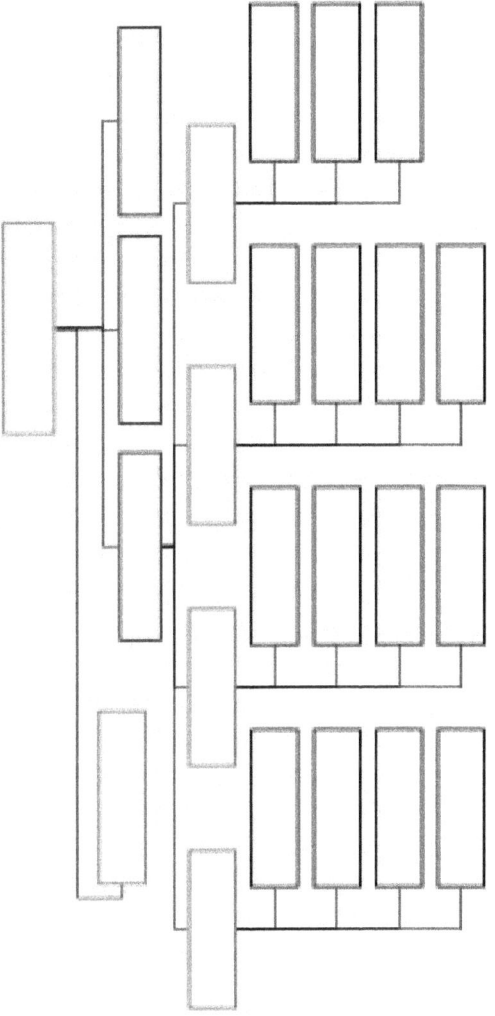

This is the proposed network and organization structure for development of the PPBC Emergency Plan.

Providence Park Baptist Church
Organizational Structure[1] for CEMP Planning

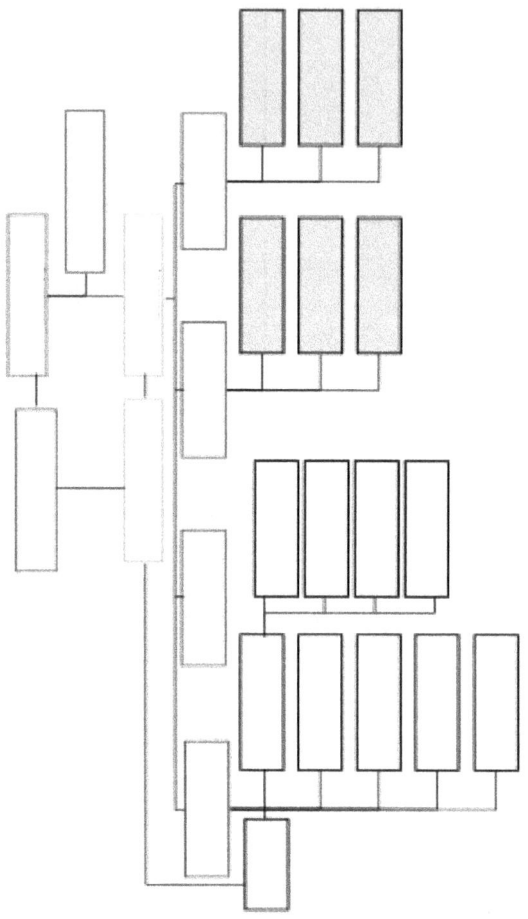

This network and organization structure is consistent with and patterned after the national model for coordinating emergency management and preparedness activities and programs with private and nongovernmental agencies.

CEMP
Emergency Support Functions[1]

- **ESF-1:** TRANSPORTATION (Bus/Van)
- **ESF-2:** COMMUNICATIONS
- **ESF-3:** FACILITY, BUILDINGS, AND GROUNDS
- **ESF-4:** FIREFIGHTING (Facility Management)
- **ESF-5:** EMERGENCY MANAGEMENT (Executive Leadership)
- **ESF-6:** HOUSING AND HUMAN SERVICES
- **ESF-7:** RESOURCE SUPPORT
- **ESF-8:** HEALTH AND MEDICAL SERVICES
- **ESF-9:** SEARCH AND RESCUE (On-Site/Off-Site Assistance)
- **ESF-10:** HAZARDOUS MATERIALS (if any, on site)
- **ESF-11:** FOOD RESOURCES (Kitchen/Pantry Operations)
- **ESF-12:** ENERGY (Facility Management)
- **ESF-13:** PUBLIC SAFETY AND SECURITY
- **ESF-14:** CHURCH-COMMUNITY RECOVERY
- **ESF-15:** EXTERNAL AFFAIRS (Church/Public Information)

1. Adapted from the National Response Framework (NRF) document, January 2008. This is the nationally recognized and recommended planning format for federal, state, and local government emergency management and preparedness planning.

CEMP
Support Annexes (SA)[2]

- Address functions applicable for all hazards
- Provide support for all ESFs
- Describe the framework to ensure efficient and effective coordination and execution of common functional processes and administrative requirements

SAs should include:

- **SA-1:** Continuity of Church Governance and Operations
- **SA-2:** Recovery Program and Plan
- **SA-4:** Financial Management (May be budget document)
- **SA-5:** Resource Management
- **SA-6:** Volunteer and Donations Management
- **SA-7:** Mutual Assistance Plan (with Sister Churches)

---

2. Adapted from the National Response Framework (NRF) Document, January 2008.

CEMP
Special Facilities and Functions

Auxiliary or Remote Sites CEMP
Address contingencies, linkages, and hazard situations requiring specialized application and coordination of the CEMP

Emergency Evacuation Plan
Describe policies, situations, concepts of operation, and responsibilities pertinent to any incident

Bibliography

Allen, Richard. *The Life, Experience, and Gospel Labors of the Rt. Rev. Richard Allen: To Which Is Annexed, the Rise and Progress of the African Methodist Episcopal Church in the United States of America: Containing a Narrative of the Yellow Fever in the Year of Our Lord 1793.* Philadelphia: F. Ford and M. A. Riply, 1880.

Baldwin, James. *The Fire Next Time.* New York: Bantam Doubleday, 1962.

"Black Churches See a Revival of Community Cooperation." *The Richmond Voice* 24/381 (May 12–18, 2010) 8.

Blackstone, Erwin, and Simon Hakim. "It Takes a Village." *American City & County,* March 2010, 40–43.

Borg, Marcus J. *The Heart of Christianity: Rediscovering a Life of Faith.* New York: HarperCollins, 2004.

Brown, Edward R. *Our Father's World: Mobilizing the Church to Care for Creation.* Downers Grove, IL: InterVarsity, 2008.

Brueggeman, Walter. *The Theology of the Book of Jeremiah.* New York: Cambridge University Press, 2007.

———. *To Build, to Plant: A Commentary of Jeremiah 26–52.* Grand Rapids: Eerdmans, 1991.

Chryssavgis, John, editor. *Cosmic Grace + Humble Prayer: The Ecological Vision of the Green Patriarch Bartholomew.* Rev. ed. Grand Rapids: Eerdmans, 2009.

"The Demographics of Catastrophe." *The Richmond Voice* 24/364 (January 6–12, 2010) 21.

Estes, J. Worth, and Billy G. Smith, editors. *A Melancholy Scene of Devastation: The Public Response to the 1793 Philadelphia Yellow Fever Epidemic.* Canton, MA: Published for the College of Physicians of Philadelphia and the Library Company of Philadelphia by Science History Publications/USA, 1997.

Frankl, Viktor E. *Man's Search for Ultimate Meaning.* New York: Basic Books, 2000.

Freedman, David Noel, editor. *The Anchor Bible Dictionary.* Vol. 3. New York: Doubleday, 1992.

Bibliography

Grudem, Wayne. *Systematic Theology: An Introduction to Biblical Doctrine.* Leicester, England: InterVarsity, 1994.

Hanna, Jeffrey W. *Safe and Secure: The Alban Guide to Protecting Your Congregation.* Herndon, VA: Alban Institute, 1999.

Hazlitt, translator and editor. *The Table Talk of Martin Luther.* With a memoir by Alexander Chalmers. London: G. Bell, 1911.

Honoré, Russell L. *Survival: How a Culture of Preparedness Can Save You and Your Family from Disasters.* New York: Atria, 2009.

Hopkins, Dwight N. *Introducing Black Theology of Liberation.* Maryknoll, NY: Orbis, 1999.

Houston, Walter J. *Contending for Justice: Ideologies and Theologies for Social Justice in the Old Testament.* New York: T. & T. Clark, 2006.

Jacobs, Mignon R. "Favor and Disfavor in Jeremiah 29:1–23: Two Dimensions of the Characterization of God and the Politics of Hope." In *Probing The Frontiers of Biblical Studies,* edited by Harold Ellens and John T. Greene. Eugene, OR: Pickwick, 2009.

Jeter, Joseph R., Jr. *Crisis Preaching: Personal and Public.* Nashville: Abingdon, 1998.

Kalmanofsky, Amy. *Horrors, Monsters, and Theology in the Book of Jeremiah.* New York: T. & T. Clark, 2008.

Kim, Susan Weller. *Hope, Help, Heal: Disaster Preparedness and Response, A Course Book for Church Leaders.* Jessup, MD: Disaster News Network, 2001.

Kim, Yung Suk. *Christ's Body in Corinth: The Politics of a Metaphor.* Minneapolis: Fortress, 2008.

Lewis, C. S. *The Screwtape Letters with Screwtape Proposes a Toast.* San Francisco: HarperCollins, 2000.

Lischer, Richard. *The Preacher King: Martin Luther King, Jr. and the Word That Moved America.* New York: Oxford University Press, 1995.

"Make Sure You're in the Driver's Seat." Richmond Police Department, 2007.

Maslow, Abraham H. *Motivation and Personality.* 3rd ed. New York: Addison-Wesley, 1987.

McDonough, Peter J. "The Demographics of Catastrophe" Online: http://www.protectingamerica.org.

McFague, Sallie. *The Body of God: An Ecological Theology.* Minneapolis: Fortress, 1993.

Minear, Paul Sevier. *Eyes of Faith: A Study in the Biblical Point of View.* Philadelphia: Westminster, 1946.

Mitchell, Henry H. *Black Church Beginnings: The Long-Hidden Realities of the First Years.* Grand Rapids: Eerdmans, 2004.

Muller, Wayne. *How Then, Shall We Live?: Four Simple Questions That Reveal the Beauty of Meaning of Our Lives.* New York: Bantam, 1999.

Musser, Donald W., and Joseph L. Price, editors. *Handbook of Christian Theology.* Nashville: Abingdon, 2003.

Bibliography

National Response Framework. U.S. Department of Homeland Security, January 2008. Online: http://www.fema.gov/pdf/emergency/nrf/nrf-core.pdf.
The New Interpreter's Bible. Vol. 6. Nashville: Abingdon, 2001.
"Neighborhood Watch Startup Guide." Richmond Police Department, 2007.
Nobles, Wade W. *Seeking the Sakhu: Foundational Writings for an African Psychology*. Chicago: Third World Press, 2006.
Olasky, Marvin. "Responding to Disaster: Being Thankful for the Days without Disaster." Address to the Commonwealth Club, San Francisco, September 18, 2006. Published in *Vital Speeches of the Day* 72/25 (November 2006) 744.
Palmer, Parker J. *To Know As We Are Known: Education as a Spiritual Journey*. New York: HarperCollins, 1993.
Peck, M. Scott. *The Road Less Traveled and Beyond: Spiritual Growth in an Age of Anxiety*. New York: Touchstone, 1997.
Pittman, Elaine. "Spirit for Service." *Emergency Management: Strategy & Leadership in Critical Times* 5/3 (May/June 2010) 25–27.
Providence Park Baptist Church. "Results of Congregational Survey." July 26, 2004.
Sanders, Boykin. *Blowing the Trumpet in Open Court: Prophetic Judgment and Liberation*. Trenton, NJ: Africa World Press, 2002.
Saylor, Jacob Lewis. *Peace Be Still . . . : Planning in Response to Safety and Security Concerns*. Centreville, VA: Union Theological Seminary and Presbyterian School of Christian Education Certification Center, 2003.
Schleiermacher, Friedrich. *The Christian Faith*. Philadelphia: Fortress, 1928.
Sinani, Gjergi. "The Courage to Be in the Philosophy of Paul Tillich." Online: http://www.facebook.com/note.php?note_id=68559588588.
Stark, Rodney. "Antioch as the Social Situation for Matthew's Gospel." In *Social History of the Matthean Community: Cross-Disciplinary Approaches*, edited by David L. Balch, 189–210. Minneapolis: Fortress, 1991.
———. "The Rise of Christianity." In *Discovering God: The Origins of the Great Religions and the Evolution of Belief*, 282–338. New York: HarperCollins, 2007.
———. *The Rise of Christianity: A Sociologist Reconsiders History*. Princeton, NJ: Princeton University Press, 1996.
Taylor, Charles. *The Ethics of Authenticity*. Cambridge: Harvard University Press, 1991
Towner, Wayne Sibley. *How God Deals with Evil*. Philadelphia: Westminster, 1976.
"U.S. Public Unprepared." *The Wirthlin Report* 13/5 (December 2004).
Vonvolkenburg, Delbert. *Keep Me Safe, O God: Planning for Emergency Preparedness and Response*. Erie, PA: Union Theological Seminary and Presbyterian School of Christian Education Certification Center, 2007.
Walker, Lee H. *Rediscovering Black Conservatism*. Chicago: Heartland Institute, 2009.

Bibliography

Weems, Renita J. *Battered Love: Marriage, Sex, and Violence in the Hebrew Prophets*. Minneapolis: Fortress, 1995.
White, Lynn, Jr. "The Historical Roots of Our Ecologic Crisis." *Science 155* (March 10, 1967) 1203–7.
Wilmore, Gayraud S. *Black Religion and Black Radicalism: An Interpretation of the Religious History of African Americans*. 3rd ed. Maryknoll, NY: Orbis, 2004.
"The Yellow Fever Epidemic." *Africans in America. Part 3, 1791–1831: Brotherly Love*. PBS Online, *1998*. Online: http://www.pbs.org/wgbh/aia/part3/3p1590.html.